MW01193923

The Place of Tides

The Place of Tides

JAMES REBANKS

MARINER BOOKS

New York   Boston

HarperCollins books may be purchased for educational, business, or sales promotional use. For information, please email the Special Markets Department at SPsales@harpercollins.com.

Originally published in the United Kingdom in 2024 by Allen Lane.

FIRST US EDITION

Library of Congress Cataloging-in-Publication Data has been applied for.

ISBN 978-0-06-343417-2

25 26 27 28 29 LBC 5 4 3 2 1

For Chloe Currens – for keeping the faith
when I lost my way

Often I see the flowers and trees of the distant sun world, but I do not see them as I used to see them. They are glowing with colour and piercingly beautiful. Their most secret meaning lies in their growth and their colour. But the people who live under the sun seem distant and small to me. With their bent heads they are running round in circles, the circles of their anxieties and troubles. Only a few of them see the glory of the sun.

Christiane Ritter, *A Woman in the Polar Night* (1938)

Contents

Prelude

The age of humans will pass. Perhaps the end has already begun, though it may take a long time to play out. If this were a Hollywood movie, the final scenes would be a man running around with a gun in some ruined city-scape, but I don't think the last people will hang around in cities: there's no food in urban areas when order breaks down. People will flee to the extremities. They will run from the chaos, disease, and killing machines to the places where a life can still be scraped from our ruined ecosystems. The last humans will, like many of the first, hold to the coast, scratching a living from the sea and the shore. I imagine the last human on earth being a woman on a rocky shoreline. I met someone like that once, a woman right at the outermost edge. A woman still living after everything she knew and understood had ended.

~

It was about ten years ago. I'd journeyed out to an island off the coast of Norway. It took two days of flights, trains, and boats to get there, and a lot of waiting around in terminals. With every transfer, the gates required

I

longer walks from the heart of the airport, and the planes got smaller. The last flight was on a twin-propeller plane. The air stewardess had to squeeze sideways past rows of oil-rig workers with puffy Arctic coats. It was May, but on the bleak coastline below it looked like the snow had just melted.

At home I was living in an old farmhouse that we were renovating, in a Cumbrian village close to where I'd grown up. I had a wooden shed out the back with a computer in it. My work was researching how to protect wild and fragile places from the growth of global tourism. My father, who had only ever worked with his hands, was confused about how that was a job, and sometimes so was I.

A few days earlier, my boss, Peter, had called. He was sending me to a place called the Vega Archipelago. The Norwegians took conservation seriously, he said, and we could learn from them.

Everything I knew about Norway could have been written on the side of a cinnamon bun, but my job was to learn fast. I discovered the archipelago was halfway up the Norwegian coast, in the region called Helgeland, on the 66th parallel, just below the Arctic Circle.

Some of the birds that wintered in our valley spent their summers on that coastline, but hardly any humans made the journey.

My destination was Vega, the biggest island in the archipelago – just a few miles long. From the boat, it seemed little more than a chain of mountain tops rising out of the sea. As we got closer, I could see there were farms and clusters of houses scattered between patches of wilderness. Two cars were waiting for passengers, and a man stood by one of them. He loaded his passenger and then asked me where I was going. He said he would take me too. After a while we passed through a tiny town with a few shops, a garage, a school, and a large wooden church. A mile or two down the road I was dropped off in a little fishing village by an old fisherman's shack, where I would stay.

I spent two days in a dull office building, watching presentations by the tourism board. I scribbled down stats and asked the questions I was supposed to ask. But I found myself fascinated by the remotest islands, and a strange tradition that seemed to keep people going out to them.

Most of the slides from these islands showed images of women. Women in little boats. Women making nests or holding eggs. Women's hands clasping ducklings. Women sitting and cleaning eiderdown. And women peering out of small wooden huts in epic Arctic wildernesses. Everything in the photos looked a little scruffy and sun-faded, like these were images of long-forgotten people from the 1960s or 70s. But as I listened to the officials speak about the women in the photos it became clear they had been taken recently. Just a few miles away, across the waves, the women were still working. They seemed to live on the rocks. In one photo, a woman had a rifle slung over her shoulder.

I had thought I'd reached one of the furthest-flung islands, but it turned out that hundreds of littler ones lay beyond it. The archipelago stretched way out into the Norwegian Sea. Vega was still civilization. Further out were places with no electric or shops or other amenities. These were the places where the women worked. Each spring, the officials explained, the women travelled out to these islands and built little wooden huts for wild eider ducks, protecting them from predators. Then, when the birds had hatched their ducklings and taken them back to the sea, the women would gather, clean, and sell the valuable eiderdown left behind. This was an ancient tradition – and it was still hanging on, if only by a thread. To do this work, the women needed peace and solitude. The authorities' job was to protect what lay beyond the horizon from the rest of us.

But, on the final afternoon, they surprised me. They said I could go for a glimpse of that world. I was going to meet a 'duck woman'.

~

I was taken out in a fishing boat with a few others. A man with whiskers was at the helm. The boat bounced across the waves, and every mile further out felt wilder and harsher, just the open sea and occasional rocky out-crops. Everyone on the boat was excited and a little nervous, like kids on a school trip.

Eventually we reached quieter water, where countless

little islands and skerries rose just a few metres above the sea, rocks everywhere. We slowed to a crawl and navigated down the channels. The man gestured to the rocks and said what I took to be the name of the place. I asked the guide what that name meant. The guide and the helmsman tried a few versions between them. The guide said it translated as 'feather island'. But the helmsman grumbled a little, and told me that his people had always called it 'the place of tides'.

Our boat navigated down the channels, winding knowingly past tide-marker poles, moving closer and closer to a tiny island, only a few acres in size, but slightly higher than the others. Beneath a little hill in the middle of the island, tucked away from the worst Atlantic gales, was a white clapboard house and some scattered red barns. This seemed to be the final outpost before the ocean. In the distance, larger waves became white as they ripped on the reef. We passed through one last channel and entered a little bay that stretched all the way to a jetty beneath the house. The man eased the throttle.

I had no great love of the sea, no romance in me about islands. My heroes weren't wandering poets enraptured with the sea. But this place was beautiful. We had arrived on a strange, watery planet. I looked around and saw a sea eagle lift from a tide pole, wafting across the waves on giant, ragged wings.

When I turned back, my companions were all staring out at a woman on the shore. Her hair was blowing loose in the wind. The tide had gone out, and she was stood on the edge of a large plateau of rock covered in seaweed – a desolate black field. She stood there, totally alone in this vast estate of rock, ocean, and sky. The flatness of our surroundings meant we could see for many miles, as far as the snowy mountains on the mainland, and back to Vega to the south. The whole coast curved around us like a giant C – a huge bay that held the archipelago.

The woman seemed tiny, like a figure in a vast painting. She was no more than five feet tall, and dressed in a woollen jumper, an unzipped fleece, dark trousers, and top-turned-down wellington boots. She was holding what looked like a broken plastic mop handle, as if to guard this isolated place. She was, somehow, hostile, like we'd strayed in and broken the order of things. My brain was searching for a way to explain this strange woman, for metaphors, or boxes to put her in. I was struggling.

She made the little hairs between my shoulder blades stand up. I was almost breathless. The guy at the wheel asked my guide, a little nervously, whether the woman knew we were coming. 'Yes,' she replied. 'I left a message.' The man looked unconvinced. I couldn't work out what this woman had done to everyone on the boat, me included. We were almost hypnotised by her. Then she took a few steps and raised her hand in a kind of welcome. The spell was broken. She was now just a woman, and we were just visiting her on a boat. I wondered what the hell had happened.

She walked across the rocks to the wooden poles of

the jetty to meet us. We glided in. Guillemots flap-splashed away across the smooth surface of the bay.

~

Her name was Anna. We couldn't have been with her for longer than an hour. She welcomed us with cups of tea and sugared pancakes, but it was clear to me she wouldn't be sad to see us leave. While the others made polite conversation, I found myself staring at her. She looked back and smiled, and I sensed, or thought I sensed, an unspoken connection.

After a while, she told everyone else to stay and finish their tea and nodded to me. She took me across the grass to show me the wild eider ducks she had tamed, sitting on fluffy grey nests in a dilapidated collection of old hen huts, barns, and abandoned cow byres. She lifted the wing of one of the broody ducks and showed me the eggs and some ducklings beneath. The birds looked anxious when I moved, but they trusted her. I said they were beautiful, and I told her as best I could about my family's farm at home. That a few days earlier I had been caring for my flock, and a raven had killed a couple of newborn lambs. She nodded gravely, like maybe we were the only people there who understood this kind of thing. We heard the voices of the others and she groaned a little. We were two naughty kids caught misbehaving, and we were about to be separated.

Before going back on the boat, I shook Anna's hand. It

felt just like my grandmother's, bony and firm. As she said goodbye, I was suddenly unnerved by how familiar she seemed. We went down to the jetty and motored away. I went back to my own life. And that should have been the end of it.

~

Ours is a dark and chaotic world. We are all in need of lights to follow. On that island I felt I had met someone who had made a life on her own terms. I was increasingly sure that I, on the other hand, had not. Not long after I left Vega, my father died. Then so did several elders from our community: men and women whom I had looked to for guidance when I was young. And, as the years passed, I began to feel unmoored, like a piece of timber drifting on the current.

The feeling grew. I worked long hours trying to succeed in a modern world I didn't like very much. I'd doubled my salary, and then doubled it again, but rarely felt any satisfaction or happiness. I was a poor husband, father, brother, and son. I began to lose faith in the certainties that had sustained me. I was growing less sure, and more confused. My work took me to places where the world was breaking; places that had, until now, survived. I saw children lying under sheets of tin by roadsides, and hospitals in slums plagued with rats and filth. Despair began to follow me home. Birds like lapwings and curlews were vanishing from the skies above our farm. I could no longer see the point in trying to mend our fields when everything around us was so broken. I had once had endless reserves of hope and self-belief, but they were beginning to run out.

Some nights I couldn't sleep. I'd lie anxiously staring at the ceiling. Part of me just wanted to escape. To run away and hide.

I couldn't stop thinking about the old woman on the rocks. There was something still alive in her that had died in me. I had seen it in her eyes. I needed to go back and work out what it was – the urge was overwhelming. It was like someone had shown me a few lines of a truly great book and then closed the covers tight shut. I had no idea how I might ever get back there.

Seven years passed. Then, one day, I wrote Anna a letter, and sent it to her via the guide who had taken me. I asked if she was still going out to work on the island and whether she might let me visit her, learn about her work, and maybe write about her. I would keep quiet, work to earn my keep, and try to stay out of the way. She replied a few weeks later to say the coming spring was to be her last season on the eiderdown island before she retired, because her health was deteriorating. She remembered me; I was the only Englishman ever to visit her. I must bring work clothes and good boots, and come quickly.

A few days later I stood on her doorstep on Vega, suddenly painfully aware that we didn't speak the same language, and that this might be a terrible idea for us both.

The Journey

The motorboat slaps and thuds, again and again, inching across the Atlantic. Anna sits in silence, a wisp of silver hair escaping from her hairband. Grey towers of rain connect the ocean to oily, black cumulus clouds. The cabin echoes with the dull drone of the engine. Windscreen wipers chug back and forth, clearing a wedge of the glass. A tin coffee pot shifts ever so slightly on its tray with each bounce. The man at the helm turns to look at Anna. She is staring to the horizon like nothing else exists.

~

Anna was much older than my memory of her. The night before, we had sat in the living room of her house in Vega. She had made black coffee, and we ate dark chocolates. Her knitting was laid over the arm of her chair. Delicate cactuses lined the window-sill. The TV was on Norwegian Ceefax – the news reduced to a few lines of text. She enjoyed watching science fiction, like *Star Trek*, she told me. This was not the half-wild woman on the rocks I had remembered. Here, she could have been a regular grandmother. I guessed she was seventy or so years old, but didn't dare ask.

We talked, in English, telling each other about our families. But we each understood only about half of what the other said, and every few sentences one of us would shrug, or laugh with frustration, and sometimes we'd give up if saying something was too complicated. She showed me her old photos, perhaps because that was easier.

Her dining-room walls were a shrine to island people. She showed me her father and his brothers and sisters, and her grandparents, several generations of the Måsøy family in formal portraits, their hard-earned affluence posed for all to see. The men looked proud, in starched shirts with stiff collars, and black woollen waistcoats and suits. The women seemed slightly stern, or perhaps just uncomfortable in their best clothes: pressed white and cream dresses down to their ankles, with their hair up, sporting ornate necklaces and brooches. These photos were taken to hang proudly on walls, in gilded frames. The women had strong shoulders, unmistakably leathery cheeks, and flaxen, sea-blown hair. The men had milky white foreheads where they had removed their fishing hats and greased their hair to the side. The outside photos showed wooden homes perched upon wild, grey rocks, and shores littered with silver driftwood. These were people recognizably like mine – people who spent their lives working with their hands, out in all weathers. They even looked like us. But my people barely ever saw the sea, and never spoke of it: they were farmers. I could feel the fierceness of Anna's pride in her family's archaic world. I had the same pride in me, and I think she sensed that.

~

That night, Anna told me many threads of stories. Some were about this little farmstead in Vega where she lived now, others were about strange-sounding islands across the sea. Sometimes a whole tale tumbled rapidly out of her, sometimes it would unspool slowly. Some of her stories were about ducks, some were about island life, and others were about trading. Some were about the early nineteenth century, others about the previous week, as if time passing changed nothing. It was a bewildering tangle, but Anna knew where each one belonged, like a weaver threading a loom. Unlike me, she could already see the beautifully crafted cloth. She wanted me to understand that her people were woven into the fabric of this place. She was the descendant of a family of 'eiderdown kings', folk who gathered and sold a rare and precious product – the feathers of the eider duck. From the north-western shores of Europe, her people had brought eiderdown to the world.

I sensed that Anna didn't accept that her family's past was dead, or that it ought to be. She carried their stories with her, like the ancient Greeks must have, long before they were written down and ascribed to a poet called

Homer. Much of her pride was about the journey they had taken, from almost-rags to almost-riches, from landless workers to people of status. All this had happened because they knew how to care for a stretch of the ocean around their islands, and how to harvest and sell the things that place produced.

As she told these stories she pointed to the old pictures on her walls. She looked like a queen – not in her clothes or possessions, but in her defiant eyes. Anna had lived a rebellion against modernity. Her belief that it all still mattered was absolute, unshakeable – a gift from God.

~

She came from a long line of farmer-fishermen: people who lived with one foot on the land and the other in the ocean. The Norwegian name for the shallow coastal shelf that stretched for up to thirty miles from the foot of the fells out into the sea is the *strandflat*. In Vega, the ocean bed, scoured and eroded by the giant glaciers of the past, poked up through the waves as thousands of islands and skerries. The water between some of these islands and islets was so shallow the locals called it the Stovelhav – the 'boot sea'; they said you could walk between them dry-shod at low tide.

As every Viking child once knew, this whole coastline was formed from the body of a dead giant. The mountains were made of his bones. The earth of his flesh. His hair draped the lower slopes of the fells with greenery.

The oceans emerged from his blood and sweat. And his teeth became the islands, reefs, and skerries. Were it not for this giant, none of Anna's family's story would have been possible. They lived in the aftermath, in the seascape he left behind.

After the ice cleared, thousands of years ago, people had worked out how to survive in this place – a mix of coastal hunter-gathering and farming. In good years, their rocky fields grew the potatoes, rye, spelt, or oats they needed. They kept livestock too. A pig fattened in the barn. A few sheep. A small hairy cow wintered on plain hay.

For many unforgiving centuries, if your barley rotted black, or the pigs got sick, your people's bellies would swell with hunger. If you lived far inland, you either starved, or you emigrated. But if you lived near the sea, you could scavenge for fish or whatever else could be caught from the rocks or the shallow waters.

Over time, those who survived on these coasts became skilled fishermen, able to go far out, where the water was teeming with fish. Giant Atlantic halibut. Huge cod with gaping mouths. Great shoals of herring. And countless other creatures you could eat, from seals to whales. Then there were the seabirds, which gave them food, including through their flesh and eggs, and warmth through their feathers.

If you could hop about this coastline in all weathers, living from rocky fields and the sea, then there was nothing to stop you spreading across all the northern seas. And so they did.

History, written by their aggrieved victims, Christian priests, dubbed the people that set out from here – to trade, explore, raid, fight, or steal – the Vikings. One of the places they left this coast for was my home.

~

I remembered a teacher at my school telling us our dialect was mostly understood in Norway. I hadn't believed him at the time, but he was right. We were the same people, divided only by a sea and a thousand or so years of history. I understood many of the things Anna said in her own tongue without translation. The list of words we both understood surprised us. Northern words, like:

Beck. Fell. Thwaite. Lowp. Sieves. Laik. Yam. Scribble.

I showed Anna my copy of the *Icelandic Sagas*, the stories the Vikings told each other about the great warriors of their time. She nodded. The sagas tell of how the Vikings took eiderdown as tribute or rent from the farmer-fishermen who stayed behind – Anna's people. The feathers found their way around the ancient trading world. As early as the Iron Age, kings and queens and warriors were buried with down blankets – some made from eider, others with the down of other sacred birds – to ease their passage into the afterlife.

~

Long after the Vikings had their day, this coastal way of life went on. Similar cultures stretched round the Baltic, across the northern coast of Russia, across Iceland and Greenland, and reached the northern territories of the US and Canada. Anna's people occupied the outer edge of Europe, on the smallest islands before the deep ocean.

Crudely, the further out you went from the mainland, and the rockier the islands, the poorer the people – but Anna's ancestors and a few others had worked out ways to prosper. They had learned to harvest the wealth of the sea and shore, fishing, hunting for seals, taking seabird eggs, and making hundreds of nests for the wild eider ducks each spring. Nests that would produce precious down, sought after the world over. For generations, Anna's family had protected the ducks from the multitude of predators which could kill them, and, when the eggs hatched and the mothers took their broods back to the sea, they harvested the down left behind in messy nests. Centuries of this work had, by the middle of the nineteenth century, made them almost wealthy, and undeniably proud.

~

I went to bed excited that night. This whole sweeping history of a thousand years or more, this whole body of knowledge and skills, survived on a handful of rocky islands thanks to a handful of stubborn old people. I couldn't wait to get out there and see the work. I lay under an eiderdown quilt in Anna's spare room and fell into a deep sleep.

~

The next morning we went down to the harbour. On a gravel track, behind a row of red boathouses, a woman was waiting. She said hello very formally, told me she was Anna's friend, and then apologized for her awful English. She was worried she wouldn't be up to the job of translating for a visitor. I was confused, and Anna saw it. Ingrid would be coming out to the island with us, she explained. I could see the discomfort on both women's faces.

There was a thud. A man was lifting bags out of a pick-up. He walked towards us and checked me out. Ingrid said, 'This is my husband, Stig. He says hello.' I wasn't sure he had said hello. But I said hello back. Ingrid enquired, 'You are married at home with children?' Yes, I replied, I had four children and was happily married. I showed her a picture on my phone.

Ingrid seemed reassured and said something to her husband. He still looked exasperated, but he nodded, and drove off.

~

Ingrid was stronger-looking than Anna, thicker-set, with glasses and straw-like hair. I guessed her to be in her late sixties. She listed for Anna the things she had remembered, and put in supermarket plastic bags, at the last minute. Anna was distracted, fiddling with the padlock on the door of one of the boathouses. We were at her family's ancestral *brygge*, or 'sea barn'. It opened and she disappeared into the shadows.

Moments later, the barn filled with light. Anna had opened the sliding doors at the other end. I saw the harbour and the headland beyond through the giant frame, and walked out on to a wooden deck mounted on stilts high above the water. Ingrid was carrying her things in from the back so I went to help her. There was an old wooden rowing boat on one side of the barn, and walls crowded with fishing gear. Long lines, hand reels, and nets hung, carefully bunched, over a timber rack. Hand-carved wooden scoops for bailing water from boats. Blue and red life jackets. And on the floor, ready to load, were all Anna's things in boxes and bags for the journey. She had left all this stuff here the previous day, before I'd arrived, in her ancient little red car, the half mile from her home.

The sea barn was like the cupboard in the Narnia stories – you had to step through it to reach the magic of the islands beyond. Out front was a carved old piece of timber with Anna's family name painted red on a white background: 'MÅSØY BRYGGE'. Other sea barns were perched all around the harbour, though some had been converted into holiday lets.

Once, Anna told me, all the farmer-fishermen had

places like this, places from which they went out to the sea or the islands. The harbour had been the hub of a bustling community. It wasn't any more. The wharfs were quiet, except for the rusty chains clanking on the buoys. The working fishing boats of the old photos had gone. It felt like a retirement village, or a museum. I looked around and shivered. The mountains behind the village were still ridged white where the snow held to the exposed elevations. On top of the mountain there was a mast rising from a radio station. The snow had melted from the farmer's fields, but his cattle were still hanging to the feeder, eating hay. The grass on the headland was yellow, matted and dead. The pine forests beyond the village and the clumps of juniper that freckled the ragged hillocks were the only scraps of green in sight. The bare birch and rowan trees caught the sun and shone like fish bones. We were in late April, and the harbour was poised between two seasons – when the sun came out it felt like the earliest moments of spring, but when it went behind the clouds the wind felt sharp, like winter might return.

~

A white motorboat chugged down the glassy water between the sea barns to where we stood. A balding man with a suntan and a checked shirt was at the wheel. He nodded a brisk hello. His name was Henrik, and he was going to ferry us out to the island. He seemed grumpy with Anna. They had what sounded like a frank exchange of opinions about how much stuff she had to load. He said, in English, that they were too old for this, and Anna said that I was strong and would help. She told him to get back on his boat and sent me to the steps beneath the wharf. Ingrid began passing boxes down to me. As they got heavier, Henrik looked at me in a way that said he loved his boat, and I'd better not scratch it. Under the wharf, slimy green seaweed hung from the timbers. Anna was soon breathing heavily, as she dragged the big boxes across the wooden planks. I asked Ingrid quietly if Anna was OK, and she said yes, but not very convincingly.

We climbed aboard, but Anna had vanished. A few minutes later she reappeared in a little yellow boat. She flicked the skin of the water gently with an oar to bring it in and dock it behind Henrik's. Out there, in the boat, she looked reassuringly young, but up close a faint dab of pink lipstick was the only colour on her. I took her arm as she climbed aboard Henrik's boat and got a shock because there wasn't much of her in the sleeve – it was like getting hold of a heron, tiny and frail inside its plumage. She must have seen my concern, because she gave me a look that told me not to say a word.

~

Henrik didn't seem to think this trip was a good idea. Someone had told him Anna had been unwell with high blood pressure. He said he had taken another woman out to a nearby island a week ago, and the rocks had been covered in ice. He shook his head. Anna glared into the distance.

Anna's bad mood seemed to deepen when we stopped at the other side of the harbour, and another passenger got on. He had grey hair and a well-trimmed beard, sunglasses, a blue woollen jumper, and a deep tan, like he'd just been somewhere hot. He looked like a healthy businessman on a yachting holiday. I moved to help him load his luggage and some fuel cans, but Anna pressed me back in my chair and smiled. The other passenger, whoever he was, clearly wasn't on our team. He tried to talk to me, but I sensed this wasn't a good idea, and would break the trust I sought with Anna. I kept it short and then sat in silence.

It was hard to make sense of all these strange relationships. I had not understood until that morning that there would be three of us going to Anna's island: Anna, Ingrid, and me. I wasn't sure if Ingrid was chaperoning Anna because of me, or if she'd have joined her regardless. She clearly admired Anna. She was scrupulously polite, but I sensed that she didn't think my being there was such a great idea.

~

We left Vega slowly, heading out past fishing lodges and the blonde pinewood frames of half-built summer houses. I recognized landmarks pointed out to me on my previous visit: the new museum with its triangular modernist roof, and the new concrete and steel jetty for leisure yachts to moor on, and beyond that the fish factory, which had closed since I had last come.

A new Norway was rising from out of the bones of the old world Anna had described to me the night before. The harbour had once been a bustling kind of service hub for the universe of little islands beyond. But that morning, as we left the harbour, we didn't see a single other human being – just a car in the distance going down the gravel track.

I felt a long way from home. The boat was soon dwarfed by the epic scale of the sky, the coastline, and the ocean beyond. We kept heading out to the cold grey sea, out from the arms of the natural harbour, with nothing but water, clouds, and light ahead. A heron was poised mid-strike above a rock pool, caught frozen in the sunlight.

~

Before long, the sea began to change around us, becoming darker and wilder. Thick clouds choked the light, threatening rain. But then the clouds thinned out and passed on, revealing patches of eggshell-blue sky. The silver chrome handrails shone in the glare of the sun. Arctic terns flitted up and down across the waves, brilliant little flecks of white.

As the minutes passed, the silence softened. Anna

played with a ring on her finger, moving it pleasingly up and down to the knuckle. I asked her what she was thinking about, and she said she was wondering whether there was enough cat food left at home, and whether her son Isak had listened properly when she told him to water the cactuses – just enough, not too much. Ingrid asked if she had brought enough pills. She shrugged and peered back at the piles of equipment we'd loaded. Bundles of kiln-dried birch logs for the stove. A propane gas canister for cooking. Cardboard boxes that had once held bananas, now packed with bags of groceries, and cartons of UHT milk, and yoghurt, and smoked salmon, and some fruit. Shopping bags tied at the handles, full of clothes. Half a dozen white water-containers sloshing and swaying. A pack of twenty-four toilet rolls. A blue plastic ice box full of clinking bottles. Plastic bags from the Spar stuffed with waterproof waders, and bundles of life jackets. Ingrid's backpack and holdall. Two 5-litre tins of paint. A cardboard box with jars of jam, pickles, and chutneys, with handwritten labels. A little plastic drum of lighter fluid. A 2:2 rifle wrapped in a black bin bag, leant carefully in the corner. And, behind us, the towed yellow rowing boat, half full of planks from broken pallets. To mend the nest boxes, they told me, which would have been beaten apart by the Arctic winter.

Looking at the pile, I realized that I was now as committed to this trip as the two women. The island was the best part of an hour across the waves, and easily cut off from home by bad weather, so we needed enough supplies. I would now live with these two strangers until July. I felt uneasy.

Until fairly recently, Anna had told me, collecting down and caring for the ducks each spring was a money-making side hustle for the men and women who lived on the little islands all year round. The rougher work, like drying seaweed, was often done by the men, but the women – fishermen's wives – had done the rest. There had been a permanent community out there, and help available if you really needed it. Now there wasn't. The women were more like swallows – wintering elsewhere, but going back in the spring, as early as possible, to make the nests. But not too early, or they'd get caught by the cold. The timing of the journey out was half experience and half gamble. If the snow came again, and it might, we wouldn't be able to work outside, and would have nothing to do but knit and shiver. If the weather became really bad, we'd be stuck out there, on our own.

To distract myself, I rummaged in my rucksack for a pen and paper and asked Ingrid the names of the little islands on the horizon. I tried to scribble them down. 'Iceland Island', 'England Island'. There was some talk about the origin of the names. But no one on the boat could agree whether these were ancient way-markers for oceanic voyages to those distant places, or whether they were where the people of those islands had been sent, as punishment for some long-forgotten crime.

~

Clouds raced each other across the sky. Ingrid asked Anna if she felt OK and got a nod in return. I couldn't stop thinking about her arm in her sleeve.

Anna had told me the night before that her grandmother, Dagmar, had lived on the island and worked with the ducks until she was very old. She'd told me this like she was convincing someone of something. She sounded like my grandfather, who had stubbornly held on to farming in the old ways as the world around him changed. It seemed heroic for a while, then sad, and sometimes almost pathetic, as his strength faded. He didn't know how to be old and let go of things. I wondered if Anna did.

She had told me about her great-grandfather, too. He sold high-quality hand-cleaned eiderdown to buyers as far away as Trondheim, sending it by post from the main island. They said that as an old man he had taken seven kilograms of down to Vega. The weight was nothing for a strong man, but the bags were bulky and caught the wind. He wore himself out lugging this oversized load across the island, against the gusts. After paying for the postage in the Post Office, he asked politely for a glass of water and a stool, and then dropped dead.

~

Henrik opened the throttle. The sea was getting rougher. The gulls riding the wind were thrown up and down by the gusts, like white plastic bags. Vega got smaller behind us. We passed through grey rain. The other passenger stood behind Henrik. They began to talk backwards and forwards.

Anna was the quietest person on the boat. She stared serenely towards the islands. When the men spoke, she listened disinterestedly. If she disagreed with something they said, there was the slightest hint of scorn on her face, or in her body language. I could tell Henrik was exasperated. But I couldn't take my eyes off her.

A sport-fishing boat passed between two distant islands. 'A tourist,' Anna said quietly. She carried on in her broken English. 'They take too many fish. There are only a few cod and they come and take them. There are no fish left in some places where there used to be many.' Henrik overheard, and said that this was 'bullshit'.

He said the big boats out at sea took huge numbers, and the local fisherman used to take many more than his lodgers took with their rods. The other passenger looked nervous and fiddled with his watch. Anna waved her hand dismissively, as if to acknowledge that Henrik was perhaps not entirely wrong, or perhaps she just couldn't be bothered to argue with him. They all went quiet again.

Anna muttered to me under her breath. What seemed to irritate her was that these fishermen had a sense of entitlement to the fish but no real understanding of how many could be taken. The new technologies not only helped them navigate the rocks, but also showed them exactly where the fish were. It was too easy. They were all taking too much, tourists and industrial boats alike.

~

To island people, fishing was like breathing. There was no life without it. Fishing and gathering eiderdown were interwoven in Anna's stories, inseparable, each impossible to understand without the other.

She'd told me that her ancestors had not gone to Lofoten, in the north, to join the crews of the big boats, as many others did. Until her father's day, they had fed their families by smaller-scale fishing round the home islands and had sold any surplus fish for cash at the trading stations on Vega. I wondered if this was because they had been affluent enough that they'd not needed to, because of the eiderdown harvest.

The great change in their lives had come as Europe's population exploded in the eighteenth and nineteenth centuries. This new, hungry world needed feeding, and fish became a hugely valuable commodity. Anna's great-great-grandfather and his sons had taken advantage of this. The islanders who lived closest to the open ocean had the upper hand over their rivals on the mainland or the bigger islands nearer the coast: in a trading age powered by the wind, they were hours closer to their catch, and more able to get to safety when the weather changed.

The busy new fishing grounds around the outermost islands ended up harbouring vast numbers of eider ducks, who fed on the by-catch and guts thrown from boats or from the wharfs and jetties. This brought masses of ducks close to the inhabited islands. In her grandmother's stories, the islands were crowded with flocks of waddling ducks that nested anywhere and everywhere. The archipelago soon sustained thousands of people, and that too was good for the ducks, because their predators were hunted, and the place was safer for them. This was the golden age of eiderdown.

But, like all good things, it didn't last. The arrival of steam, and then motorized boats, emptied the oceans of fish. These new boats could carry a much larger catch, and keep it chilled for longer, taking it down to bigger harbours to sell. There was no restraint. They cleaned out the fisheries around the islands and pursued the remaining fish further and further out into the Atlantic. The ducks were drawn away with them, desperate for scraps. The natural wealth that had lifted Anna's family out of poverty was ebbing away. This was the beginning of a slow decline that would take a century or more to play out, eventually driving the islanders to Vega, or to the mainland, or further away still. It would take all her family's skill and hard work to survive on their island, and to keep a decent number of ducks coming back to nest each year.

~

The waves were now cresting, white horses above the green-blue ocean, and it occurred to me that if anything happened to this boat, we'd all be dead in a few minutes from the cold. I began to look more carefully at the sonar screen that Henrik was navigating by – digital greens, yellows, and blues flickering to show the depths. A dozen or so dotted lines on the screen showed his previous paths through these waters, ghost journeys, digitally remembered.

The island where we were headed, Ingrid said, was surrounded by such shallow, rocky water that the tourist fishermen in small boats stayed away. It was too dangerous for them – they took one look at their sonar and turned back.

Even for those who know them, the islands are dangerous, Anna replied.

~

The family stories Anna grew up with were full of the drowned. Sad stories that merged and tangled in my head. Anna's great-grandmother Louisa had lost four sons and one grandson at sea, all in separate accidents. The first two sons were strong lads in their twenties, experienced seamen. They went out fishing not far from home but were caught by the 'fall wind' – gusts that came down the face of the mountains on Vega. The wind pushed them off course and capsized their boat. When a search party went out to look for them, all they found was a stain on the rocks, the herring oil from their catch. A third son drowned while fishing near the island of Bremstein. And when, some years later, a fourth son, along with her seventeen-year-old grandson, didn't come home from a fishing trip, Louisa knew straight away they were dead. She had a dream that night about where her grandson would be, and woke the next morning knowing he was in the water near an island they called Lurøy. She persuaded her husband to sail her there. It was so cold she wore five skirts, one on top of the other. They found the boy's body swept up on the rocks. They carefully wrapped him in one of her skirts and took him home. His father's body turned up down the coast in another municipality a month later. A little while after that his widow and their children left for America.

The church on Vega has a plaque with the names of those who had been lost at sea. As a girl, Anna said, she had looked at it and recognized many of them. Whenever the grown-ups got together for coffee, their talk would always turn to the folk who had died on the way out, or back, across those short stretches of ocean. Many of the men who went up to Lofoten fishing for cod in winter never came back. In some of these coastal parishes one in four men died at sea. Her father had drilled into her the need to be careful. If you didn't take the sea seriously, you should stay on Vega and feed the cows.

In an emergency, the women would hang clothes on the flagpoles to get the attention of passing fishermen or other islanders – a sign to come and help. But help often came too late. When someone died, the singing would begin. It was the tradition to have a 'singer for the dead': someone who sang with the corpse in the home, while people came to pay their respects, and who would keep singing as they went across the waves, taking the body to be buried on Vega. They wouldn't stop until the priest took over the singing at the church door.

~

I traced my finger across the paper map on Henrik's table, trying to find the names of the islands from the stories Anna had told me, but the map was dotted with hundreds of islands and islets and they all looked the same. I'd read about the Sami people and wondered aloud whether they came this far south on the mainland. Anna pointed to some jagged mountains to the north.

'They still go there in the winter with their reindeer,' she said.

The Sami would come to Vega for the winter from time to time, she told me, their herds of reindeer swimming out across the sea to nibble on the wilder bits of the island for a few weeks.

Then Henrik began to tell me all about his lodges and his boats. He was a survivor, keeping up with the times. He'd discovered that groups of guys with money from places like Germany would pay well for a fishing trip, if you made sure they had a good motorboat and all the fishing gear they'd need. They wanted to come home to a warm and tidy lodge each night with a fridge full of beer. Henrik put it all together. He seemed impatient with people who wouldn't move into the future, and he looked at the women, sat quietly behind us, doing nothing much. Suddenly I felt tired. Henrik tried to tell me more, but I didn't encourage him, and he soon fell quiet.

I was starting to feel that I'd been unwise in coming. I'd rushed around before my flight, working myself almost to exhaustion so I could take this time away. Somewhere in me, I knew it wasn't fair to disappear from the farm and leave my family behind; but, for the first time in my life, I didn't care. It wasn't just that I was tired. I was lost. I'd begun to avoid other people – just speaking to others emptied me out. I felt overwhelmed, and angry at everyone around me. I was in trouble, and I didn't know what to do about it. That was why I'd been drawn to Anna. She had seemed so happy – so sure – out there on her island, on her own, away from the demands of other people. Even when we'd got onto the boat, despite the men's irritating presence, she had seemed almost entirely self-contained, radiating a sense of purpose and sureness. But, very occasionally, her magic flicked off – like her batteries were fading – and she seemed old and small. And, in those moments, doubt flooded into me.

Things would feel different once we were there, I told myself.

~

Jerry Lee Lewis was hammering away at his piano. I was brought back to the boat by the music. Henrik tapped

33

his hand on the wheel and sang along. He had a pile of discs in the cupboard by his elbow, all American. Anna smiled at him, lost in the music. He wore a checked shirt with a grey T-shirt underneath, and aviator sunglasses in his top pocket. His forehead was freckled and peeling. He'd been on holiday in Lanzarote, Anna whispered. She said that he had no right to lecture her about being 'too old'. Then she pointed to three dots, half a mile away, on some rocks. Seals, speckled grey and white, curled up at each end like bananas. One of them wriggled nervously to the water and stopped, half submerged.

I sensed the mood on the boat had changed. Everyone seemed excited. We were approaching a vast raft of rocks that seemed to stretch for miles. The islanders were heading home.

We left the open water and began to pass isolated islands. First was one with a stubby tower painted like a lighthouse. Then another with lengths of timber thrown up its rocks by the winter storms.

Then we passed alongside another, which looked like an old, grey battleship that had been torpedoed and rolled over on its side. I went to the back of the boat. The sun now caught the water, making it shine a deep purple, like gloss paint.

Islands and skerries were rising all around us, dozens of them, like the backs of a pod of whales. Soon the open sea was just a memory. The tide marks on the rocks reached four or five metres above the water. The higher reaches had only the most cautious tint of green, like the grass had only just dared peak out into the biting winds, after the ice and snow.

We sailed on towards bigger islands, large, cold and grey in the distance. A giant metal sea-mine rested on one of the headlands – a relic of the war.

'They took the dynamite out of it to use in the mines in the mountains,' Henrik explained.

Soon they were all chipping in with war stories. The Germans had occupied the whole coast early in the Second World War, but the soldiers sent here seemed to be mostly remembered for how they drowned.

Henrik told me that two Germans stationed out on Steinan Island, near the lighthouse, saw the fishermen's children play *dragsug*. It was a simple game: you got as close to the outflowing waves as you dared, and then ran back up without getting your feet wet. The soldiers decided to play themselves. They dared each other to go closer. One of them misjudged a giant black wave and got pulled away.

Ingrid told me that, one day, a group of German soldiers had appeared, searching for an escaped prisoner the resistance had hidden on another island called Flatholm. The others all nodded like this was one of their favourite stories. The islanders there helped smuggle weapons from English boats to the resistance, and the Germans didn't trust them. They'd been watching Flatholm from far out on the ocean and had seen the prisoner. But when they came in and berthed, there was no man. They searched the island's barns and duck huts. An old couple came out of the house protesting, and the Germans told them to shut up. The soldiers were almost at the last unsearched duck huts when there was a commotion back at the house. A German officer had a man at gunpoint – except it wasn't a man, it was a middle-aged woman dressed in men's clothes. They shouted, why was she dressed like that? She said she always worked in her husband's clothes when he was away fishing, they were comfier, and it was safer if people thought a man was home. The officer had been furious – this must have been who they saw. The soldiers left, embarrassed.

Once they had gone, the prisoner scrambled out from beneath the final duck hut. When the woman, whose name was Kristina, had come out of the house, the Germans had been only a few feet away from discovering him. She had used her wits to save his life. The other passenger on the boat said something in Norwegian, and I got the impression that this story related to him, somehow.

Anna said the farmers on Vega had sold the Germans rabbits for meat on the black market. But the farmers on one of the islands cheated and sold one of them a skinned cat. The German soldier figured out he'd been conned and was furious. 'No more cat meat!' he'd shouted.

Everyone on the boat laughed.

~

Anna was switching on now. These little islands and rocky skerries were like those she had gone out to as a child

36

with her father, she told me, looking for driftwood and picking cloudberries. When he found valuable timber, he dragged it up the foreshore, above the high tide mark, which meant it was claimed as belonging to them.

If a rock rose above the waves and had anything of value on or around it, that meant someone had claimed ownership of it. The places where you could fish, hunt for seals, gather seabird eggs, or simply pick cloudberries were governed by written and unwritten laws like these – laws that went a long way back. The whole archipelago, she said, gesturing to the map, had claims on it from different people. Anna's father would erect crosses on the headlands of their family's islands to let other people know they were 'pacified' or 'sanctified' – Ingrid tried a few explanations of something called *fredlyst*, the system by which they applied to court for this protection, but we soon gave up trying to understand. Thieves still regularly came out and took timber or seabird eggs. Her father knew the signs, and often who it was, but never managed to catch them red-handed.

I looked at the map but saw only a confusing tangle of what might have been contour lines. The map and the seascape around us seemed to have nothing in common. The lines on the paper were meaningless to me, so I abandoned my efforts to decipher them. Anna simply explained it instead. This – the rocky plateau we were pulling towards – was one duck station. Beyond it lay another, the one we were travelling to. The ocean and islands were, she said, divided into a series of *vær* like these, each one a little cluster of islets. Ingrid tried to find an English phrase for this and struggled. We settled on 'sea estate', but Ingrid said there was something that wasn't quite covered by those English words. The Norwegian word emphasized that these were places that things could not be taken from without permission and, in a country where roaming and harvesting from the wild is usually allowed, this was an important distinction. There are many sea estates, many of which had harvested eiderdown in the past, but now it seemed you could count the remaining duck stations on two hands.

~

These invisible property lines clearly meant a great deal to islanders, just as the ownership of fields or grazing land mattered deeply to my people. Each *vær* was like a tiny independent kingdom. They were, Anna explained, often separated by petty rivalries and feuds. There were endless quarrels and tensions about who did things properly and who didn't, who took too many fish, or who had the rights to this or that outcrop of rock. They were commercial rivals, but also after the same eggs, or driftwood, or fish. Duck women took great pride in the quality of the work on their patch, in doing things right. They judged each other harshly.

Each *vær* was unique, as different as the stars in a galaxy. Each island – and even each islet – had its own history and character, dictated by such things as how far it was from the mainland, just as the distance from the sun made planets suitable for life or made them burnt or frozen. Some islands had fresh water and safety above the storm waves and were habitable; others weren't. Some islands offered the chance of a good life; others offered only hardship and poverty. Some islands were like extensions of the mainland, with grazing just a short boat-crossing from a farm, barely islands at all. Others, like Skogsholmen to the north, were little farming communities, rolling green hills rising from the sea, dotted with sheep and cows. Some, like Bremstein – Anna pointed to the horizon – were far out, near the deeper water. They had had barracks for fishermen, to save them the long journeys home. They were somewhere to thaw until the storms passed. That island had a quarry, a cod-liver oil factory, a railway to the concrete wharf where bigger boats could dock, and a giant stone break-water to protect the harbour from the waves. There was a whole village at Bremstein perched on the rocks: boats pulled up the beach, women cooking, children playing, fishermen mending nets on the shore, and a warren of wooden houses with chimneys smoking. These island histories reminded me of home, where hundreds of small farmsteads had once littered the hillsides; each had been its own world for the people that lived there, each must have felt timeless and eternal, and now almost all were gone.

~

The colours changed on Henrik's sonar screen, the dark blue vanishing as the ocean floor rose. We had entered a new seascape, surrounded by acres of flat rocks and seaweed, none of it higher than perhaps twenty feet above the waves. He was more focused now, peering ahead and nudging the helm this way and that. It looked like we might run out of water soon. In front of us there seemed to be an unbroken raft of stone between the ocean and the now blue sky, full of fissures and cracks and little channels. In the distance there were a dozen or more houses and barns, like a village, perched on the surface of the rocks. They were tidy and well-painted – red, white, and grey. The passenger fidgeted and looked at his watch.

I whispered to Ingrid, 'Is this a duck station?'

'Yes . . . Flatholm.'

'Does it have lots of ducks?'

'Yes, once . . . Many people lived and worked here . . . And then none.'

The whole place looked precariously flat, as if a giant wave could sweep across it and smash it all to kindling. Henrik eased the throttle and guided the boat round the skerries and into a channel leading to sea barns and timber wharfs jutting out across the water. The passenger was gathering his bags. On a red sea barn hung a neat and varnished pine sign: 'Velkommen til Flatholm'. The water sloshed and gurgled as the boat moved. A few feet above the tide, on the wharf, were black crab pots, a stack of four white plastic buckets, and a wheelbarrow.

The man said something to Henrik as he docked with a rope thrown down from the wharf. A dark-haired woman appeared above us. She shouted 'Hello' down to Henrik. She wore a green top and was younger than Anna and Ingrid. She was the man's wife. They said something to each other as he got to her level, and they giggled. The woman peered down, trying to make eye contact with Anna and Ingrid, and sent another 'Hello' echoing into the cabin. Ingrid said 'Hello' back, and Anna's lips moved too, a little, as she mumbled something, but she had disappeared far inside herself. I couldn't catch her eye. The woman gave up and scolded her husband play-fully for something or other he had done wrong. She talked loudly to Henrik. Ingrid whispered a rough trans-lation to me. She was telling him how many nest boxes they had already set out. I wondered if the report she gave Henrik was actually meant for us, the neighbours and sort-of rivals, or if it was perfectly innocent. Anna seemed unimpressed, but she was perhaps just tired. After a minute or two, Henrik said we must press on. The last timbers were handed up. The husband shouted to us all to come and visit. But the way he said it, and the older women's muttered reply of thanks, suggested to me that no such journey would ever take place. And then the man, his wife, and their things vanished into the sunlight.

As Henrik came back into the cabin, the two women were looking at him. He shrugged as if to say 'What?' then shook his head and pulled the throttle on the engine. Behind Henrik's back Anna was smiling wickedly. Ingrid gave her a stern look. As we glided quietly out of the channel, I saw several carefully placed wooden boxes dotting the headland. Each box had a neat little sliding door pulled open at the front and was weighed down with heavy rocks. They might have been made by a carpenter. Anna was studying them too. Ingrid told me that this duck station was very well organized, and we had a lot of work to do to be at the same stage of readiness for the ducks. Anna said the ducks had not come yet, there was plenty of time. There were no prizes for making nests too early. She waved her hand as if brushing away the very existence of the suntanned businessman and his chatty wife, and their freshly painted houses. These neighbours were the descendants of proud duck people, Henrik told me, but they lived in the south.

~

With the man from Flatholm dropped off, the mood on the boat was lighter, almost giddy, the worries of earlier in the day replaced with enthusiasm. We were close to the island that would be our home and workplace for the spring. I asked Anna where it began. She nodded to a little rocky ledge that we were passing.

'This side is Flatholm . . . beyond is Fjærøy.'

I said that the distance was tiny. It looked like a gentle swim might get you from one sea estate to the other.

Henrik grinned and said he wouldn't recommend it.

The small tidal channels had currents that would sweep a swimmer away like a length of driftwood.

I sensed it wasn't just the currents that made swimming between the two duck stations a bad idea. Apart from Henrik, no one on the boat had any interest in going from one side to the other.

~

I knew from the night before that Anna's family *vær* had been hard won. They had lived and worked on the islands for as far back as anyone could guess, but they were poor and didn't have title to the land. For many centuries after the Viking kings had left, their lives would have altered little. Their island home was owned, in turn, by large aristocratic estates and by wealthy merchants from as far away as Denmark or Sweden, when 'Norway' was little more than a province of those countries. To these affluent men, Norway was like the American frontier, a Wild West full of virgin forest and plentiful fish, inhabited by backward peoples like these islanders and the Sami. A place to be exploited. Vast areas further north ended up belonging to wealthy landowners, and they'd hire the local people, most of whom were poor, to extract everything of value whether it was sustainable or not.

In the early nineteenth century, a new law forbidding outsiders from claiming what was not theirs brought the Vega islanders a degree of emancipation. Islanders could now petition a court for protection of the places that sustained their livelihoods – making them, effectively, the legal stewards. Anna's great-great-great-grandfather Halvor petitioned to have the new law applied to his duck station, staking his claim to protect, and harvest from, his small parcel of land and sea. People from afar, he said, insulted him by shooting seals and otters, collecting eggs and down, digging his fields, and taking firewood without his permission. All while he was paying good money in rent to harvest these things from the *vær*.

The petition was granted, his family's stewardship of those rocks and acres of ocean now upheld by the law. But they remained tenants. Proper freedom meant owning your own land, your own *vær*. Buried in the new legislation were a few lines that said that tenants could purchase their land if they raised enough money – but few could afford it.

Anna's proudest story from the night before was that her great-great-grandfather Harald had bought their sea estate in 1852. He had outwitted the landlord by turning up to a meeting on Vega and triggering the purchase of the island. Anna said the landowner had a high-pitched voice. He'd apparently coughed and spluttered that these islanders couldn't possibly have enough money. Harald laid the full amount on the table in cash. He had quietly built up funds by selling fish and eiderdown, being careful to keep his dealings under wraps and let the landlord believe he was poor. Harald left that meeting as the owner of his own *vær*.

Anna had told me this story like it was from the Bible. It was the 1920s before some of the neighbouring families got freehold of their islands. Owning their own island meant Anna's family had a certain status, and accrued the level of material wealth on display in the portraits she had shown me.

Harald's children, Anna's great-grandparents, built up their *vær* until it was home to 1,500 eider-duck nests each year. Given the modest size of their sea island, just a few acres of rock, this was remarkable. The whole place must have been blanketed with ducks. They got as much as twelve kilograms of down in the best years: enough for twelve whole eiderdown duvets. Each one was worth 30 kroner in the markets at Brønnøysund and Tilrem, almost as much as a cow. They called eiderdown 'islander's gold'.

Anna said they made so much money one season that they bought a 24-foot sailboat outright. But their growing wealth didn't equate to respect back on Vega. The stigma associated with outer-island life was too strong.

This was made apparent every Sunday, when, like all islanders, the Måsøys would attend church on Vega. Norway was a deeply Protestant country, with a powerful church. People here worshipped a hard God, sang watery hymns and read psalms about fishermen. Their Messiah calmed storms, walked on water, fed people fish. They loved stories like the one about Jonah and the whale. Attendance at the weekly service wasn't optional – there was a fine for those who didn't turn up. The established Vega families sat at the front, in the posh seats. Anna's family and the other outer-islanders had to sit at the back and come in through a different door.

They sailed across rough seas, sometimes a four-hour journey, only to be insulted.

The islanders said the priest on Vega was a hypocrite. He drank too much – often, his horse had to get him home – and saw nothing wrong with this segregation. But Anna's family were defiant: they created a stir each week when they arrived dressed like they were as wealthy as the folk at the front. Her grandfather wore a shiny gold watch on a chain pinned across his chest. Her grandmother sat beside him in silence, furious at this social snub. Their eiderdown wealth had upended the order of things, and no one knew what to make of it. But, however much money they made, their status didn't change. They remained back-of-the-church nobodies.

Everything and everyone on this boat was, I began to realize, wound together in Anna's threads of island history. It was all a pattern that dated back centuries. A history of stigma and defiance coloured her relationships with us all: Ingrid, Henrik, the businessman – even me. The other passenger had committed the grave sin of seeming to be a wealthy southerner – nothing he did or said after that made a difference. Henrik was just another man telling Anna what she could and couldn't do. I almost felt sorry for the two men, but I held my tongue. I was here for her, not them.

I sensed Anna had a use for me beyond being an extra pair of hands. She wanted me to know about her people and their past. She had built herself out of the old stories, as had each generation before her, and now those who told them were dying out. Sometimes, in the days that followed, if Anna told me a story and I didn't scribble it down she would look at me like maybe I hadn't understood its importance, and would glance at the paper as if I ought to record it.

~

The water around us was turquoise. I could see flashes of the bottom of the channel, dotted with smooth, round boulders.

The main island in the sea estate of Fjærøyvær was called, simply, Fjærøy (pronounced Fi-aroy). We took the last mile to our destination slowly, the boat winding between the skerries. Henrik stared carefully at his depth-finder screen for rocks. They seemed to me too close, like they might easily rip the bottom of his boat out. But no one else appeared concerned.

Ingrid pointed to a series of giant mountain peaks on the mainland far behind us, the Seven Sisters. They were once beautiful women, she said, the daughters of the troll king of Sulitjelma in the north. One day they escaped from their father's control and danced naked on one of the islands. Anna and Henrik began to disagree. He said the maidens had been swimming naked in the sea. Ingrid tried to hold firm. She said a giant called Vagekallen had seen the troll maidens and had been overcome with lust. He chased them on his horse, and they dashed away. Amidst all this chaos and nudity, the troll sisters had forgotten the golden rule: they must not be touched by sunlight. As they fled, the first fingers of the rising sun turned them all to stone.

North of these peaks, Henrik said, there was a giant mountain that resembled a man's face, the Dønnamannen. He had been turned to stone, too, in the same raunchy troll story, but nobody could remember what he'd been up to.

North of that giant face, towards Bodø, I could see a distant mountain range too gothic to be true, like a pencil illustration from an old copy of *The Lord of the Rings*.

Henrik turned to Anna, but she was looking intently at the island before us. Then he smiled to Ingrid, as if to say, 'Here we go again.' But Ingrid too was lost looking ahead. He shrugged to me instead. In front of us, there was only one family of islands left before the wild Atlantic.

Fjærøyvær.

The Place of Tides.

This was the edge of the coastal shelf, the *strandflat* – the end of it all. There was nothing beyond these last few little islands but the deep, dark sea, and, somewhere out there, nine hundred miles away, Iceland, and beyond that, Greenland or Newfoundland. We left the last channel and entered the last bay. Anna sat up straight. She was back where she belonged. She smiled as she scanned the rocks for familiar, workaday things I did not yet know to look for.

Henrik idled the engine. Little black guillemots tumbled into the sea from the jetty and pattered across the waves, their feet striking the surface like tiny pairs of castanets. The swell from the boat lifted rafts of yellow seaweed by the wharf. As the water around us shifted from black to deep blue to aquamarine, I could see the sea floor: white sand and broken seashells. Ribbons of kelp swept around the hull as it drifted in closer to the timbers.

We docked and clambered up. As Henrik and Ingrid began unloading, Anna gestured to me to follow her up the wooden boardwalks away from the water. The main island wasn't big, no more than three or four football pitches. Its highest point perhaps fifty feet above the sea. Alongside the path was the red sea barn, like a large garden hut. Anna unlocked the padlock on the door and shouted something back to Ingrid. Then we went up a goose-nibbled path, past some chicken coops with corrugated tin roofs and wooden fronts. On our left was a rotting grey barn, where Anna had shown me ducklings when I first visited.

A stranger passing this island, coming in from the sea down the deepest channel, might think it was a tiny community – and it once had been. Home to a family, plus ten or more fishermen who had billeted in the barns. But now there would be just three of us in this lonely, beautiful place.

The shadows cast by the barns lengthened down the hill. The sun had passed the peak of its late-winter arc, and the day was fast dying. Anna said there was a lot of work to do. The paintwork on the clapboard house in front of us was cracking and flaking. This was where we would live for the season.

It all seemed a little forgotten about, and cold. Shards of grey roofing sheets crumbled by the barns. The doors on some of the duck huts were hanging on broken hinges.

The raw sea winds had held any vegetation in check, leaving the island stuck in the end of winter. The remains of an old pump engine, flywheel and shafts, sat on the headland, rusting. A wooden bridge had fallen into the gully beneath the house. The floor had collapsed at one corner of the barn they called the Firehouse. Buoys were thrown in the grass. Tangled fishing nets lay half-submerged in vegetation. Old boats were beached and rotting on the foreshore. Fjærøy still looked much like it would have done a century ago – if slightly more chaotic and ramshackle.

Anna unlocked the door. It smelled a bit musty, but seemed to breathe as she opened into the living-room and the tiny kitchen. Ingrid arrived after us, her brow shining with sweat. She said the bags and cardboard boxes were unloaded from the boat. Anna and I looked through the living room window and saw the mountain of stuff on the quay beside the roof of Henrik's boat. I went back down with Ingrid. We loaded the wheelbarrow together, in silence.

~

Anna had built a fire in the stove from a bucket of kindling. She splashed it with lighter fluid from the squeezy bottle, and then flicked a match. A minute later it was roaring, and she added logs. A few minutes after that the stove-top fan whirred gently. Ingrid was unpacking dry goods in the pantry, still not saying much.

The fire lit, Anna beckoned me to the back door. She pulled her coat tight against the biting sea breeze and walked ahead. We wound through an abandoned garden, past a series of duck huts made from boxes and old oil barrels, over a ravine on a wooden walkway, up a crooked path past more duck huts, and onwards, up the hill in the middle of the island.

When we reached the top, I couldn't help but gasp.

To the west, the rocks ripped white gashes in the Atlantic swells. Giant breakers hissed spray up into the sky, and it danced down the wind for a hundred feet or more. A vast panorama swept around us for miles. Skeins of gulls beat hard in Indian file from north to south. Anna smiled at me, at my silent awe of this landscape. I felt a surge of adrenaline. It felt good that Anna had got back here, for her last dance. In the cold light she looked ecstatic, like the energy of the whole ocean was flowing through her veins.

There was only one jarring note in my head. The photographs she had shown me the night before did not seem to have been taken on this island. The buildings that stood behind her great-grandparents, her grandmother, and her father, uncles, and aunts in the photos were different to those we'd just walked past.

I asked her how long she'd been in charge of the island.

'Fjærøy? Twelve years.'

The question mark in her answer confused me. Perhaps sensing this, Anna said,

'Måsøyvær before that . . . I am from Måsøyvær.'

'What? Like your name?'

'Exactly, my name . . . we are from that place.'

'You're from another duck station? You are named after another island?'

'Yes. The island is named after us. I am from Måsøyvær.'

Questions formed and dissolved in my mind. Anna looked towards the south and pointed across the sea, a little to the west of Vega. 'Måsøyvær,' she said. Then she turned and walked back to the house.

I stayed on the top of the hill, taking it in.

The setting sun painted a highway of icy white across the ocean. It started out at the horizon and passed over the waves, up the rocks, through me, and back to the snow-capped mountains on the coast, the spine of Norway. Those blue fells stretched all the way to Sweden.

Night was coming. Ingrid was struggling with some bags we'd forgotten on the jetty. I knew I must go and help. Anna had paused on the lower slope of the hill, looking at something. Henrik's boat was pulling away, out and across the still water of the channel that led back to his home. Jerry Lee Lewis echoed out across the bay in erratic waves of noise.

2.

The Choice

Ingrid picks her way slowly across the rocks. She is wearing a thick woollen jumper and what might be her husband's trousers, held up with a belt. I follow her. The rocks are treacherous, with big fissures, so she reaches down to steady herself and tells me, without looking back, to watch I don't slip. I look across the water to the Atlantic in the distance, over a series of little bays. A sea eagle stands on a skerry just across the water from us. Its feathers gleam yellow, like burnished gold. It holds a large fish in its talons and rips at the pink flesh with its beak. The silver scales and porcelain-white fishbones shine against the dull, dark green of the seaweed. The eagle sees us. It lifts its head, then continues tearing at the fish.

The Norwegian flag flaps half-heartedly behind the house, the wind clanking the rope against the aluminium mast. I follow Ingrid down to the foreshore. The ocean is calm – the deepest indigo.

We are walking the boundaries of our tiny island, checking the state of the nesting places. I wonder if we are also showing ourselves, so the wild things know this is still a duck station.

Soon the foreshore beneath our feet is covered with

fragments of sea urchin shells, hundreds of curved shards – pink, white, and mother-of-pearl. This hillside on the back of the island is littered with triangular duck huts and piles of stone and planks. There is also a strange box, which I guess must be a trap. There are drifts of rotting seaweed and timber lying here and there. A grey hut is perched on the lichen-covered rocks, 'Trondsen' painted on its front. Ingrid opens its wooden door, and peers in. She seems to be looking at the floor, then picks at the seaweed in some old nests. She shuffles the door back into place and shakes her head. The big sky above us is a beautiful watery blue, but Ingrid says the nesting structures are too damp and the weather forecast is not good. We must wait before starting the work.

~

The first sound I'd heard that morning was the floorboards creaking as Anna got out of bed and walked along the landing. The second was the ladder-stairs groaning as she climbed down. Then the kettle rattling on the gas hob. A little while later, there was the rusty squeak of the stove door. With those same sounds, in that same order, the house would stir every morning for the next ten weeks.

My bedroom was in the eaves at the northern end of the white house. The beams across the ceiling were draft-proofed with old ropes caulked over the cracks. The first night, I pulled my sleeping bag around my neck, but still woke up cold. It was, I realized, much warmer to share a small room – as Anna and Ingrid were doing.

On my way up I'd seen the two bunks in the room where Anna and Ingrid slept. They were like those you'd find on a ship, a narrow gangway between them, beneath a window looking out to the sea. A golden icon hung above Anna's bed – a Bible verse in Norwegian beneath it. From Mark, I would later learn: *Not what I will, but what thou wilt.* Jesus was on his knees among the rocks, praying to his father, surrendering to his fate and God's mercy.

I'd woken at 2 a.m. and thought I heard the seabirds screeching. The wind seemed to shake the little house. I looked out of the window and saw just dark rocks in the sea mist. It was gloomy, like the grey sky was resting on the ocean.

I lay awake for an hour thinking about Anna on the hill. From here to Vega, and then across to her family's island, there was a giant triangle of ocean, a few miles long on each side. Anna's whole life seemed to have taken place within it. Despite all she had told me, the furthest point was a mystery, the island that had given her family their surname. I put on a jumper, and then fell asleep again.

~

In the morning, I made my way downstairs. Our living space consisted of the kitchen and the living room beside it. There was no running water, and no bathroom to speak of, just a compost toilet in a hut down the path. Through the open door of the living room, I saw Anna washing her face in the porch. She had filled a bowl with water from one of the white plastic containers, and I understood that this would be where I would wash and brush my teeth, surrounded by pegs laden with our outdoor clothes and trying not to fall over our boots. There was a tiny mirror hanging from the window latch. She was not embarrassed by any of it. She soon had a mouthful of froth, shoved open the stiff back door, and spat over the fence into the grass. I followed her out the door. She told me that the first spring she came here, she had struggled to push this door open because the wind was so strong. Other times she had opened it to deep, packed snow. From where we stood at the end of the house, I could see three sea eagles hanging about on the tidal-marker poles. This had been their wild place all winter, and now they seemed sulky and reluctant to leave. Another must have been on the roof of the house, because it swept over us on big lazy wings. Anna clapped her hands sharply, and it did one half-anxious wing beat, then carried on.

Anna looked pale and tired. She said it was always hard work to come out, but now she could rest, get her strength back. Back in the kitchen, I offered to help with breakfast, but she shook her head and pointed to a chair at the table. The kitchen had a sash window with six panes of glass. Each was like a little painting of the bay and islets below the house, and the mountains in the distance. I drank the coffee she poured me and looked out. The ocean light changed by the minute. The dead grass on the headland was buffeted in the wind. There was a pair of binoculars next to Anna's porcelain cup, like she had been studying something out there. I asked her what things were called, and she pointed to plates and cups on the table and tried to teach me their Norwegian names.

~

Anna made beautiful breakfasts every day. She laid out each item like it was a kind of ritual, placing everything with great care. The first morning I wondered if the spread was for my benefit, a guest to be impressed, but as the days passed it became clear this was just what she did.

She'd reach up to a little shelf crowded with muesli, flatbreads, biscuits, sugar, coffee, and bags of nuts, and bring down a packet of brown sugar or the coffee. She cut slivers of smoked salmon into a saucer, where they curled in the sunshine like rose petals, and glowed pink. She carved slices of bacon on the worktop, then laid each thin strip down in the sizzling pan. On the second of the three gas rings she cooked pancakes one at a time, which emerged brown and freckled with old fat, and she folded them into quarter wedges and layered them in a white enamel bowl.

~

The bacon was crackling and spitting in the pan when Ingrid came in with her hair unbrushed. She asked if I had slept well, then began helping lay the table, taking out a carving knife to cut the cheese. She said the knife was blunt. Anna seemed irritated by that but said nothing. The morning light poured through the holes in the lace blind, hanging halfway down, sending duck-shaped crochet shadows across the linoleum floor.

When the table was laid, the two women sat down. Anna spread a pancake with brown sugar and bacon fat. She pointed to the food and told me to eat. I wasn't sure where to start. I cut some brown cheese and tried it with the salmon, and some plum jam on a crispbread. As I crunched through it, I could feel Anna staring at me. I said, 'You don't eat these things together, do you?' and she started giggling and said, 'No.'

Ingrid fiddled frustratedly with a knife in the jar of honey to get some on her bread. It had dried on the sides of the jar into sugar granules that sparkled like glitter, and when she ate her bread it crunched in her mouth. She opened a yellow plastic pot, full of assorted teabags. Anna grumbled that the lid didn't shut properly anymore. She said 'Lars' had been messing about with it when he was last here. He must have broken it. Lars was the carpenter who worked out on the islands, Ingrid explained. She found the herbal teabag she liked and hung the label on its string over the side of her steaming cup.

The house had a Sunday-morning feel to it. I asked Anna what we would do today, and she seemed confused.

Half an hour later, in the living room, I asked again with different words. Ingrid heard, and said we could go and take a look to see what might need doing around the island. I imagined the three of us would head out, but Anna sat down in her chair, as if making breakfast had exhausted her.

~

Later I'd see the patterns and understand the season, but in those early days I felt lost. I had no idea how the work would unfold, what came first, what later, and why. I didn't realize it then, but the first part of an eiderdown season was simply getting to the island, making the house warm, and cooking plenty of good food. Spring would creep slowly up the Norwegian coast, from island to island, and this year seemed to be dragging her heels. After Ingrid and I got back from our short walk round the island, the rain came. The women settled in to avoid getting wet. I was impatient for something to happen, but they did not seem troubled by this waiting. They said it was how things were here. There would be plenty of rushing around when the place dried up. Rain pattered on the glass. The logs in the stove crackled. The two women chatted whilst they knitted on the sofa by the window.

The tides crept in, and then ebbed away.

I was left to take a 1970s-style leather chair. Over it were sprawled sheepskins that Anna told me she had made from her own sheep back on Vega. Anna and Ingrid chatted in Norwegian, and I tried to drop back into the shadows, determined not to be a nuisance or a disruption. I read *Moby Dick*. Occasionally they'd make a coffee and ask if I'd like one. Anna looked at me from time to time, over her knitting, with what seemed to be curiosity and amusement.

~

Later, Anna and Ingrid began to quiz me about my children. I said my daughter Bea was helping to look after our farm, and that she was a proud girl. Anna said she had been like that, too, proud of her family's work. She had not grown up on her family's island, on Måsøy, but everyone on Vega knew that that was where she was from. One day, she'd gone to the village shop with her sister. An old woman recognized them, and said, 'Ah, you are the Måsøy ducklings' – and the nickname had stuck.

As she told me this, I could see that the island had given her and her siblings more than just their name. It gave them their identity.

'What happened to your family's island?' I asked.

~

The wind was rattling the windows. I loaded the stove basket with logs. Anna responded to my question by telling me a story about her father as a little boy.

He had been an island kid. Growing up, he had barely left Måsøy. But when he turned seven, he was forced to go to school on Vega. After the boat had dropped him off and turned back towards Måsøy, he had stood on the jetty with his head bowed, desperately sad.

Ingrid looked forlorn, as if that little boy were in the room with us now.

Anna told the story of that homesick little boy like it explained everything, like such a snapshot or moment of great feeling eclipsed a thousand pages of history. But as I listened to it, and others that followed, and pulled at the threads, a bigger story emerged. We talked for hours that day, and then the next, as rain showers passed over the island. From time to time one of us would go to the back door and look out or trudge down the sodden path to the toilet hut. Sometimes Anna seemed to have had enough of speaking and we would sit in silence. The women would knit and I would read. Anna would ask me about my sheep or cows, or how I had met my wife. And I would ask her questions. We wandered to and fro through her family's past, sometimes into what felt like dead ends, but then always turning back to continue the story. From time to time, Ingrid would see my confusion and would press Anna to explain something. Sometimes Anna would get lost in a story, forgetting about the here and now. It took a while, but slowly the threads made something bigger. We started with a homesick little boy and ended up in an epic tale about how the archipelago, and the whole world, was transformed.

~

Anna's mother and father left Måsøy in 1946, two years before Anna was born. It had been a beautiful day when Frederik and Ulka had packed their boat with all their things. Anna laughed with Ingrid as she told me that her three-year-old sister Gerd had hives from eating too many seabird eggs, after the plain food of winter.

Her father was the last brother to leave. The abundance that had made their family wealthy on Måsøy had vanished. Fewer ducks were coming each year. By the 1930s the family were making half as many nests as they had in the glory days. The value of the eiderdown masked some of this decline, and had just about upheld the status of Anna's grandparents, but the hard truth was that the islands needed fewer young men.

There had been eight brothers and sisters, and one by one they had tried to make a living on Måsøy and failed. One brother tried farming sheep. Another built a cold store by breaking ice in winter and storing it, wrapped in hay, for fishermen to store their catches until they went to the mainland. But the fishermen didn't come, and when the ice melted he left, too. Before long they'd all gone to Vega, or to the mainland, or beyond, following whatever work they could find. It was hard, but they'd come back to fish or to stay whenever they could. The sisters left to get married, all except the eldest, who stayed with her mother.

The brothers were among thousands who left in search of work. The latest wave, in a long series of waves that swept people away. There were islanders who went all the way to America, and settled in places like Minnesota and Wisconsin, drawn to familiar-looking rivers and lakes, and pine forests. They built Norwegian-looking red barns on their Midwestern farms, or were hired on American fishing boats, because few people knew the sea better. Those emigrants wrote wistful letters home, full of island-longing.

One daughter from Flatholm, Anna said, had gone to New York. She became a housekeeper and sent money back to her family. They'd write to her for help whenever someone got diphtheria and needed a doctor. Many years passed. Then, one day, she returned to visit, now an old woman. She seemed incredibly wealthy to her island relatives and neighbours. But their lasting memory of her would be how, decades after leaving, the island was still the most precious thing in her life.

~

Anna's father had actually left the island before he married, before the war. He had gone to study at the maritime college in Trondheim. He qualified as a helmsman and fell in love with a farmer's daughter: Anna's mother. They married. Anna said her mother had been nervous about going out to Måsøy to meet his family. She was from Vega, after all, and outer-islanders had a reputation for being a little rough. But his family were welcoming. They fed her hearty meals and gave her a light eiderdown duvet. She thought she would be cold because she had only ever slept under a heavier felted-woollen duvet, and in the morning she was amazed how warm eiderdown was. Then the war came. The German Occupation in 1940 made it sensible for the couple to stay on Måsøy. You could earn very little money there, but you'd not go hungry if you could fish.

There was no escaping the war. The archipelago became a rat-run for the Resistance, who smuggled people, information, and weapons in and out. The fishermen could rendezvous far out in the deeper water with British warships or submarines. Some younger island men in the Resistance fled to the Shetland Islands to escape being caught. There, they rallied to the cause of the Free Norwegian Government, and some even went to London to meet their exiled king. The women and the old folk stayed and said the men had gone fishing. The Germans grew increasingly suspicious. They searched for radios and weapons. The whole coast became a fortified frontline. They built barracks on Vega, and Anna said the oldest islanders could still remember running errands for them on their bikes as young boys.

Certain islands were identified as being strategically important. A gun emplacement was built using slave labour on the neighbouring island of Ylvingen, to keep

Royal Navy ships from getting too close to the coast. The Germans wanted to get to Måsøy, too. They tried to make one of Frederik's brothers navigate them to the island from Vega, but he mugged them by guiding them down a shallow access-line. When they saw the rocks ahead they chickened out. They shouted and bawled at him, but he said it wasn't his fault, the water was too shallow. They backed out to the safer deep water. And so, for five years, Anna's parents, her aunt, and her grandparents hunkered down on their ancestral island in relative peace, only going to Vega for supplies when they had to, under cover of the white flag that would keep the Germans from sinking them.

~

Through the window, Anna spotted a little white boat far out on the water, heading from right to left, and we all watched it pass. She knew who it was, but I couldn't catch the name. Then she got up, crossed the room, and lay down on a bed in a corner alcove. She seemed lost in thought. Above the bed was an ornamental ship's wheel, with a picture on its hub of a steamer belching out black smoke, and 'KRISTIANIAFJORD' written on a ribbon round its waist. There was an old painting of a man staring off into the distance, with a Roman nose, wispy grey parted hair, and a far-seeing gaze, like a Navajo wrapped in a blanket. Anna caught me looking at him. He was Roald Amundsen. 'He beat the Englishman Scott to the South Pole,' she said, with a glint in her eye.

~

As Anna told me about the war, Ingrid would chip in with details, or would say she hadn't told the story quite right, and they'd bicker about some detail or other. Sometimes they'd be unsure of the facts and would say they must ask Lars when he came, as he knew more about the Resistance. But the moral of almost all their wartime stories was that the islanders had chosen the right side, and had been both courageous and resourceful. An island people who had spent centuries scavenging from the sea were quite capable of hustling under an Occupation. They stole whatever they could from the Germans, and there was a thriving black market. They had salvaged from the wreck of a British fighter plane pulled up from the seabed, using the aluminium for bailing cups and casserole pots, and for years afterwards Anna's father had worn the pilot's glasses for goggles when he was breaking rocks.

But there was no denying that island life was hard. These were lean and hungry years. To try and make some money, Anna's father had gone with other local lads to work for the Germans on a railway in the mountains on the mainland. Just two weeks later he came back. He wouldn't work there any more, he said. Something had happened. He looked troubled. Later they learnt that he'd worked on what was known as the blood road, where slave workers, prisoners of war from Poland or Russia, died in horrible conditions. He never spoke of it again.

~

When the Germans left, the islands were among the first places to raise the Norwegian flag, but the war had turbo-charged the long-term decline of the archipelago.

At the beginning of the Occupation, the Germans had noticed the thousands of half-tame ducks swimming around the islands. They didn't care what kind of ducks they were. They didn't care about eiderdown. And they didn't care what the locals said about them. To the Germans, a duck was a duck. The eiders were chalked up as food supplies for the Third Reich. Used to feeding on the fish scraps given to them by the islanders, the ducks were not scared of people. This made them easy to catch with long nets. Anna's people held the ducks in almost sacred esteem – they never ate them. But now the waters around the islands, long protected and policed, became a duck-killing zone.

By 1945 there were no longer enough ducks. On Måsøy they now only made 400 nests – a century earlier it had been three times that. Still, Anna's grandparents clung like limpets to those rocks. When his children spoke about leaving to start a new life, her grandfather would leave the room. He said some of the people taking on the islands were no good. They let the duck stations decline. They stole seabird eggs. They were greedy and took too many fish.

I told Anna this proud old man sounded like my grandfather, and she asked all about him and what he did in the war. He had stayed on his farm, I said, and traded eggs, butter, and fuel on the black market. He once told me about being in the Home Guard and sitting on a ridge surrounded by sheep as the skyline flashed, because the Luftwaffe was bombing the shipyard at Barrow-in-Furness, far over the hills. He remembered hearing the engine drone of the empty bombers as they headed home.

Anna looked deeply sad. Her grandfather had died in late 1945, she said. Then her parents moved to Vega.

Her grandmother held on for two more years with the help of her eldest daughter, and then she, too, loaded her things into a boat and left.

Anna said her parents had argued about where on Vega they would live. It was only a question of a couple of miles here or there, but it mattered to them. Her father wanted to move to the village he knew from his school days, looking across the sea. But her mother insisted they go inland, to the farming village she was from. They could live on her family's land, called Steinbakken – 'the rocky place'. She wanted to be closer to her mother, brother, and sister, especially since his job as the helmsman on a well-boat, carrying live fish, would keep him away at sea for long stretches. She won the argument.

Years later, Anna's father told her that her mother's

farming family were 'rich' by comparison with his own. It must have been hard, I thought, for the son of a once-proud eiderdown family to move into his in-laws' backyard.

The home wasn't much – a barn that could be lived in, on a few acres of plain, stony land, half a mile from the harbour. There was a kitchen and small living room downstairs, and two bedrooms up a flight of tiny wooden stairs. Through a door from the upstairs bedroom there was a hay loft, and below that were the cattle and sheep. The family could hear them at night, munching in their stalls. Downstairs, a door in the living room led straight into the barn, where, in the winter, the chickens lived in a stall.

The cockerel woke them up each day. Anna and her twin brother Tore were born in that barn-house in 1948. The same year that the island life of her family came to an end.

~

Late that day the rain stopped. Anna went out, and I followed to help. She inspected the larger duck huts. One had a door that needed mending. Another had a wooden front that had rotted and crumbled. She disappeared into one of the little barns to fetch her tools, but came back empty-handed and said she was too tired. She returned to the house, where Ingrid was making fishcakes and boiled potatoes. I paused on the headland and watched an oil tanker crawl slowly across the horizon.

~

That night I lay in bed listening to the wind and the waves and the oystercatchers' piping. I tried to make sense of what Anna had told me – of what had happened to her family's world. It was shocking how long ago the decline of the ocean had set in. The Germans had decimated the ducks, but fish stocks and seabirds had been ebbing away for a long time before then – and with them, seemingly, the viability of island life. This place hadn't magically escaped modernity. If I had come for that, I had followed a fantasy. Anna was born, lived, and worked in a broken world.

I knew what that felt like. As a teenager, I'd been told our family farm was finished. I hadn't accepted that, because I loved it. Even now, years later, against all the difficulties we were facing, I was doing everything I could not to give it up. We had never sold our fields or moved away; I grew up on that land. I wanted to make a life for my family there. I loved my father and grandfather and the fields they had worked too much to do otherwise.

I knew all about pride and defiance. But Anna's story was even more extreme. She had barely known her grandparents' world: it had just about died the year she was born. Somehow, though, she was still out here seventy years later – and fiercely attached to it.

If the ducks had been wiped out, how had she managed to keep the eiderdown work going? And why wasn't she doing it on her family island? Anna preferred talking about the golden age of her people, or about anything at all, to talking about herself. For me, she was the story, but there were whole chapters of her life missing.

~

The next morning was much like the first. From my seat in the kitchen, I watched three geese swing over the headland in formation; they spread their feet and splashed down into the bay. It looked overcast again. Soon, big raindrops tapped on the windowpanes at the back of the house.

Anna laid brown cheese on wholemeal bread spread with butter, added a dollop of plum jam. Her face looked pale, and she fumbled at the little hinged lids of her pill box. She sipped water from a Coca-Cola bottle on the table to down her pills. Ingrid had not yet emerged.

I felt restless. I found the switch from my manic, rushing-around life to this quiet life unsettling. I was raring to get work done on the island at the same pace. I wanted to do jobs for Anna, like chopping wood or carrying things to the house. I wanted to do those tasks quickly and well, to earn praise by being useful.

Perhaps sensing that I felt cooped up, Anna said I could go out on my own wherever I liked until the ducks came, though I must not use the rowing boat. So, I wrapped my scarf around me, put on my thick jacket, and headed out into a seascape of greys and blacks. At high tide, there were only a few small acres that I could walk around, much of it fissured and cracked slabs of rock. I was learning that our dreams of islands as places of freedom and escape are fanciful – an island is defined by constraints and limits.

My world was now dictated by the coming and going of the tides. Fjærøyvær was a family of hog-backed islands rising from the water, some of which I could walk to across causeways, or, at low tide, across the seaweed, but others – only a few oar-strokes away – were out of reach. This place was perfect for creatures like otters that could run and swim, ranging freely across it all. But I could not do that – my world stopped at the water. Soon the island was shrouded in cloud, or sea fog. A giant black raven, its neck feathers ruffled, passed over me and honked.

My daydreams of this place had all been of the outdoors. But I was now aware that, when it rained, we would be housebound, and it might rain all spring. The kitchen and the living room would feel very claustrophobic with three of us stuck in there for weeks. It seemed to me that such a place would either become your everything, or it would drive you insane.

I walked to a sea barn by a sheltered inlet, opened the door, and peered into the darkness. I stepped inside and had to crouch to avoid hitting my head on the wooden boats hanging from the beams. One had broken free and its remains were crunched up in a corner among the seaweed and lengths of timber. The rest of the barn's contents looked like they'd been tumbled inside a giant washing machine.

I kept wandering. I looked in another barn, this one on land, and made out what might have been a bunkhouse, with a loft for a fisherman and his family, and a workshop below. I wandered to another small barn and opened it with difficulty. Inside was a table strewn with yellowing newspapers and magazines, like it hadn't been touched since someone had left in the 1940s. Anna seemed to be living among the ruins of what had once been, working in a relic seascape, crowded with ghosts. Then the showers came, half rain and half sleet, and I was glad to get back inside to the stove.

~

The women were knitting. Anna looked brighter and asked me what I had seen on my walk. We sat quietly after that, for an hour or so. I read my book.

The rain beat on the windows and the wind howled, and eventually we settled further into our places in the scruffy old living room and began to talk. I asked Anna how – and why – she had become a duck woman. And I asked her, again, what had happened to Måsøy. And Anna, again, began to weave an answer, starting from an unexpected place.

~

When she was six years old, Anna's family moved in to a new house across the yard from the barn they had lived in. Her father had earned enough to build them a beautiful wooden house. He had worked on it his every waking moment, when he wasn't away on the fishing boats. Anna had helped him, passing him tools and carrying planks. Her father painted it white. You could see it shining out from the road.

In the new home, Anna and her twin were given separate bedrooms for the first time. But Anna hated sleeping there. Everything felt new, like she might break it. She missed her old bedroom, the familiar smells, and the cockerel crowing in the morning. So, one night, she moved back into the barn. I laughed, and asked what her family made of that, and she said they simply accepted it. They knew how stubborn she was. Tore loved his new bedroom and teased her for moving back. But she didn't mind. It was where she wanted to be.

~

I liked the sound of that rebellious girl who wouldn't bow to anyone. But, as she told more stories, I began to see that that wasn't quite the point Anna was making. It was something else – almost the opposite.

For much of her life, Anna had been deeply ordinary. She had mostly conformed to what the world wanted, and built one kind of life – a modern, respectable one – but had never completely let go of the other. It was only through extreme wilfulness that she had found her way back at all.

~

The Anna that I knew, the rebellious duck-woman, had taken a long time to emerge. Still, the spirit had been there, inside her, bubbling up, ever since she was a girl listening to her grandmother's stories. Anna told me her grandmother, Dagmar, had been stubborn like her. She hadn't sold the island when her husband died. And she refused to give up on the ducks, even after she moved to Vega. It sounded to me like she had travelled back to Måsøy to make nests each spring. Just like we were doing now, but sometimes I found it hard to follow Anna's explanations.

I asked her if she had gone out to work with her grandmother as a little girl, but she seemed surprised by that idea. No, she told me, she had only seen the islands in high summer, on school holidays. By then, most of the ducks had gone back to the sea.

From time to time, her grandmother would come to stay with them in the white house. Her aunt, with whom she now lived, would drop her off. Anna said the old woman wore a black dress with white flowers and an apron. She got terrible headaches and asked Anna to massage her hair with turpentine. She cleaned eiderdown in the basement. Anna's mother told her she wasn't to go down there, because the air was dusty. But she'd crept down anyway, because her grandmother told strange, dark island tales in which everyone seemed to drown. Anna's mother said the old woman shouldn't tell a little girl such morbid things, but it made no difference. Anna kept going back. She learnt about ducks, and down gathering and cleaning, and about the islands back when they were filled with people making their living from the sea. She fell in love with the outermost islands through those stories. They were steeped in her grandmother's nostalgia for people who had left. Anna wanted the world of those stories to be alive, and to be hers. She daydreamed about living across the sea, about doing the work her grandmother had done.

It sounded to me like Dagmar had shown her that there were different ways to be a woman – she was quite unlike other 1950s housewives. When it came to the island, the ducks, and the eiderdown, her grandmother and great-grandmother were the bosses. But the idea that Anna herself might be that kind of woman was buried with her grandmother in 1964, when Anna was sixteen. In Anna's stories, her grandmother was like a time traveller from a bygone age. When she died, that age and that choice seemed to vanish, too.

Anna's options were more prosaic and domestic. Her schooling had fizzled out. An operation on her eye the previous year had left her unable to read for a while, and disrupted her final months of secondary school. Her father said more schooling was a waste of money. Girls might as well be at home learning to cook and clean. Her mother said this was nonsense. Anna's older sister Gerd had qualified as a nurse and had a job in the old people's home on Vega. She got Anna a holiday job there to pay her college fees and her mum helped. Anna signed up for something called Housewife School, and went there for a year, and then she did a year at the Folk High School. After that she had to find work, which usually meant going to Oslo or elsewhere in the south.

Her brother had gone to university and became an engineer in the oil industry. He moved south, married, and had four kids. Anna's parents proudly hung a picture, in their living room, of one of the oil rigs he worked on in front of a glorious sunset. But Anna had no dreams of leaving. The old people's home said there was full-time work in the kitchen for Anna too, if she wanted it. There weren't many other options, so she took it.

~

However remote, islands aren't outside history. They are deeply affected by it. By the time Anna was old enough to leave school, the eiderdown islands had changed almost beyond recognition. For decades, government policy had focused on moving people off the islands and to the mainland, or biggest islands, as part of an ongoing project to drag these 'backward' people into the future. The old farmer-fisherman way of life, even with eiderdown to sell, couldn't generate wealth like modern industrial life. Islands had no electricity, were too far from the new jobs and the schools and hospitals.

The North Norway Plan, launched in 1951, created a system by which islanders were paid to relocate and scrap their small fishing boats. The young were encouraged to leave for university or for jobs in the south, or, later, the oil rigs or big new fishing boats in the north. The old folk left behind were encouraged to settle in the larger island communities, like Vega, or, better still, move to the mainland. Anna told me that several families on the little islands had accepted the money and left. Her family had left before the policy and had been paid nothing. The payments created bitterness and arguments, because people who wanted to stay would be undermined when others took it and left. Some islands needed populations of a certain size and enough young people in good health to get the work done, or everyone had to leave.

In the 1960s Norway discovered vast oil and gas resources beneath its ocean bed and modernized with breathtaking speed. Finding oil reserves at Balder, and later at Ekofisk, changed everything. The country was soon stitched together by roads and railways, with modernist bridges and concrete tunnels through the mountains, and regular ferries waiting at every stretch of water. Everything connected and punctual and centralized.

A new Norway emerged, and the outermost islands with their archaic ways weren't part of it. The stigma Anna's great-grandparents had faced in church as backward islanders was now government policy.

Vega became home to many of the people who left the smaller islands. It had deeper soil and was home to farming and fishing villages where there was work for some of the men. But many others had gone further afield to start new lives, sometimes hundreds of miles away. Plenty still kept ownership of their islands, but could only come back for holidays. Anna was lucky in this respect, she said, pausing her knitting. They had left, but they remained only a boat journey from their home island.

The population of the archipelago had halved in her lifetime. As recently as the mid-1960s three or four hundred people lived on the outer islands. Now Henrik's brother was the only one left, she said.

~

When Anna told me that she'd gone to 'Housewife School', I'd raised my eyebrows – I'd never heard of such a thing. It seemed funny that such an independent woman had been earmarked for domestic training. But Anna said the school taught her lots of good stuff – including agronomy, how to run a farm. They grew vegetables, made cheese, and learned how to mend clothes. And yes, they'd also been taught how to host a dinner party. They had sewn their Bunads, too — the embroidered folk dresses, specific to each region, that Norwegian women wear every 17 May. Anna's was green, with ornate silver catches on the front, and embroidered with red, yellow, and blue flowers.

But, she said, they also taught the girls economics. And when they got to the end of the year, a teacher told her not to marry a boy until she had seen his pocket-book. If he was stupid with money, she should not marry him.

Anna wanted me to know that she had been content when she was younger. She went to parties with friends at the Youth Club House. They listened to folk music, and some boy always had a harmonica. In summer they'd have bonfires and people brought food. The older lads brought moonshine liquor and the nights would some-times end with fighting and chasing girls.

She had met a young man called Bernt. He worked for the telephone company and serviced the cable car which went up the mountain to the radio station on Vega. They married in 1969, when she was twenty-one years old. They soon had two boys, Anders and Isak. Perhaps they'd married too young, or they just weren't right for each other, but after eight years they called it quits. He went to work on Svalbard in the north. She was a single mum, proud of her sons. She carried on working at the old people's home, her parents looking after the boys during her shifts.

Then, some years later, Anna met Henning. He was

tall and handsome with sandy hair, and loved the sea and seabirds. He was the policeman for Vega and the outermost islands. When the town had its 17 May procession, with flags and drums, it would end up at the nursing home. Henning was one of the men at the front, with the mayor and the other grandees. Anna was on the little balcony with some of the old folk, wearing her bunad, and they'd smiled to each other.

Before too long, they were married. Henning built them a wooden farmhouse on a rocky headland, and the field below it stretched down to the beach. He kept sheep on his family's fields. They had two daughters together, Mari and Amalie. Anna's sons had already grown up and left home. She planted forty rose bushes round the house. Henning carved two beautiful, ornate wooden beds for the girls. Anna was living an ordinary life as a wife and mother. She said she was happy.

~

So far, there were almost no ducks in this story. I pushed her, asking what had happened to the eiders in the years after her grandmother died. Well, Anna replied, a few had continued to nest on Måsøy, and her father and her aunt went out during springtime in alternate years. The two siblings had inherited the island between them, on the basis that all the older siblings had made new lives, and the two youngest had stuck around and helped: Anna's aunt had inherited the house that was the island's main residence, and her father got the sea barn, which he made into a place for his family to stay. In the holidays, Anna's mother would sometimes send her with her dad to keep an eye on him and to help him with the work. Mostly, he'd focused his efforts on preserving the island's houses and sea barn with fresh coats of paint. But he did what he could with the nests near the house and the sea barn, too. It sounded like he'd taken Anna out there with no great expectation she'd ever take duck work on herself. But this was the beginning of an island apprenticeship.

Anna told me her father was a quiet man, always jobbing around the place, tidying up or making things in his blue boiler suit. He was home a lot between fishing trips, which was how he'd had time to build them their new house. After he'd finished that project, her mother hadn't wanted him under her feet on the farm. She had sent him to milk the cow once and it had jumped, kicked over the bucket, and run away. She said his hands were too rough, and that was the end of that. He'd ended up going out to Måsøy a lot – gathering driftwood, hunting, fishing and harvesting wild seabird eggs.

~

The first time Anna ever saw an eider duck was with her father. She had gone out with him to Måsøy, to an island in the *vær* that her father called Grasholmen – 'the little grassy island'. They were looking for driftwood that had washed ashore in the winter. He told her to stay away from the shoreline unless they were together. Mines from the war were known to turn up on beaches, and she might be blown to kingdom come. He wandered off a little way and she watched the waves. Then she heard a strange noise coming from the rocks. She called to her dad, and he came back. The noise was a duck trying to persuade her ducklings to come out of the seaweed and onto the water. Six or seven grey, fluffy ducklings, no bigger than her own hands, tumbled around, falling between the rocks. Anna was desperate to catch them before they got to the sea, afraid they might drown. But her father held her arm. We must leave them, he said. She had cried, not because he was gruff, but because she was scared – they were too delicate to be out on the wild sea. The mother called, and, one after another, the ducklings followed her. Her father said, 'Watch, they will float, you will see,' and they did. They were tossed around by the waves, but somehow stayed glued to their mother's side. Gulls were screeching above in the blue sky. It seemed a miracle that these babies would survive. Anna watched as they bobbed away across the water.

~

Anna's father had said he wanted to save his children from the heartache he'd felt as a child, the pain of losing an island, and so he'd moved the family to Vega. But it seemed to me that those were just words. He had never stopped going out to Måsøy, never stopped loving the place and caring for the ducks, and trying to keep that world alive. Whatever the North Norway Plan said, many of the people who left the islands kept going back. After Anna's father retired on a sailor's pension in the 1970s he thought about little else but his beloved island, and was rarely away from it for long.

As Anna talked, it was clear she had been far more influenced by what her father did than what he said. Her father was the reason that their island and its eiderdown traditions had survived, until it was her time. It was through helping him that her own love of the place grew. He knew the sea and the islands in a deep way. She loved learning about the birds and other wild things from him. One day she thought she saw a strange new stone wall on one of the skerries towards Bremstein. She told him, and he said the sea played tricks on your eyes.

'Take the binoculars and look again.'

She did, and the wall turned out to be moving and alive. Hundreds of seals crammed on a flat rock.

~

As Anna spoke, I watched her face. She seemed to be living the memories as she shared them. Ingrid hung on her every word.

But after telling us about her father she didn't want to talk more, and I felt I had tired her out. I said I was sorry for all my questions. She said it wasn't the talk, but her blood pressure. She seemed angry at her own body for letting her down.

~

Later that afternoon, Ingrid made coffee. Anna prepared a simple meal using the things we had brought that would not stay fresh much longer. The bread rolls and cooked meats were spread on the table and we picked among it all and chatted. I said that the Anna in the stories she told of her early life almost sounded like another woman, a fairly conventional housewife with a job as a cook. I was surprised by how 'normal' she had been, a far cry from the half-wild duck woman I'd first met.

Anna said that, back then, the only experience she had of the duck islands was through her father and the trips out with him. But after a while those trips became almost impossible. Life just got in the way. There were seasons she had not been able to go with her father at all.

Anna usually spoke matter-of-factly, but as she talked about this time in her life, she seemed to falter. She went to the kitchen and washed the cups. Later, I asked her what it was like to go to their island, when she got those rare moments. She said it was heartbreaking that there was no longer a family home. The place felt increasingly derelict and unloved. It was horribly quiet. Even the flowers had been dug up and taken to her father's and aunt's gardens on Vega. Despite her father's efforts, the once-proud duck station with its hundreds of nests was slowly falling into disrepair.

Then there were the eight dead ducks hanging on the quayside, she said. They were seared into her memory, even though it was fifty years ago. She was close to tears when she told me about them. She had gone out to the island with her father, and, as they approached, they'd both seen them hanging from a rail on the quay. A relative was staying in the house, and had found them, strewn around a hut, the previous day. He'd hung them up so Anna's father could see. Little downy feathers blew across the foreshore. Her father took himself away across the grass. Anna hadn't seen him cry before.

Until she saw those eight bodies, she'd never believed the ducks were in real danger. Though their numbers had dwindled since the island's heyday, there had always been some still coming. They even nested in the sawdust beneath her father's workbench in the old barn, and next to the block outside where he chopped logs for the fire.

The mink changed that. They'd been brought to the islands back in the 1960s to be farmed in cages for their fur. They were fed fish scraps and were, for the islanders, a nice little earner: a bundle of fur to sell along with the eggs and eiderdown, helping to pay the bills. Then the mink had escaped and started breeding in the wild. By the late 70s they were everywhere, like a biblical curse. They would turn up on an island and kill every last eider. Mink could swim for miles and had no natural predators. The ducks had no chance.

The government paid a bounty for each mink killed, and Anna's father set traps. But unless someone was constantly watching for, and trapping, mink, they could not reduce their numbers enough. It was impossible to protect the ducks without living permanently on the island. The mink would sneak in when you had gone home.

From that point on, the duck numbers crashed, until there were almost none nesting on the main island on Måsøy. Her father kept going out, and kept making nests, but by the late 80s they went largely unused. The way Anna told this, it seemed like the ducks had trusted her family for protection, and they had let them down.

~

A terrible sense of guilt awoke in Anna. But she couldn't do anything about it. She was so busy with the girls. And she had commitments at the nursing home, too. She had worked as a cook in the home for thirty years. She was proud of that work: it mattered to her, and she was good at it. She kept a clean and well-organized kitchen and, as instructed, stayed largely out of sight of visiting relatives. She rarely took a day off for illness. She made the old people traditional meals they loved, like dried codfish with white sauce and potatoes, as well as cakes and cookies.

From her kitchen window, she could see across from one leg of the H-shaped nursing home to the other. The curtains were usually open, so she could look right into the rooms of some of the old folk, and the common room where many of them sat watching TV or being cared for by the nurses. She kept one eye on everyone, making sure they were OK. At Christmas they would decorate the spruce tree outside with fairy lights, and on Christmas Day she'd bring in her daughters with their presents.

I said the old folk were lucky to have someone caring for them like that. Like they were family. Yes, Anna said, there had been many good times, and she had done her best.

But sometimes, on bad days, when she stood at that window, she began to feel like she was in prison. She fed the little birds crumbs and watched them hang on the feeders. Once, she saw a large cat kill and eat a sparrow. Anna wished it had flown away and escaped, but it had seemed strangely entranced by the cat until it was too late.

~

Anna told me several stories about the old people in the nursing home before I realized that she was saying something vital about her journey to being a duck woman. These weren't just any elderly people – they were some of the last islanders. The last generation to have been born and raised in the old way of life. They'd wanted to tell their stories, and needed someone to listen and care. That person had been Anna.

She talked to the old fishermen about the sea that they would never go back to, giving them the news from the harbour. With shaking hands they told her of their time on the boats, fishing up north, and where they'd gone hunting for seals or harvesting seabird eggs for their families. Their whole world was still out there, beyond the headlands, beyond the rocks, beyond the harbour and the jetties. She knew that if their bodies had allowed it, many of the residents would have sailed back to the islands before nightfall. And Anna began to wonder why she didn't.

~

Anna's father grew older. He still went out to Måsøy to build nests each season, but it was a token effort – a stubborn holding-on. There had been 1,500 ducks in her great-grandparents' time, 900 in her grandparents' age, less than 400 after the war and now there were just a few. Occasionally, Frederik found the remains of a duck near the nests he'd built – another bird killed by a mink. Sometimes they swam through the little bays and inlets, but warily, as if they'd worked out that the main island wasn't safe. He had to go out to the skerries and outlying islands to harvest some down from wild nests.

Then, one day, her father had an accident with an axe. Luckily, Anna's brother was on Måsøy with him. The old man had cut himself, and he was a bit shaken by the time they got back to Vega. The doctor came and said the wound would soon heal, but his island days were over – it was too dangerous. Soon after that, he moved into the nursing home where Anna worked.

Anna would check on her father several times a day. One moment her father would be himself, sharing wisdom with her about the sea, and the next he'd become a bit confused. Worrying about him kept Anna up at night. And she felt sorrow for the island, and for the ducks, completely unprotected now without anyone to look after them. Maybe it was time to come to terms with reality: it was finished.

~

A museum was built on Vega and Anna went to see it one day. It was all about the duck stations, the women's work, and the eiderdown tradition. Something about it had fired her up. She liked Inga, who ran the museum, and it was good to know her people and their work weren't forgotten. But she saw a stuffed eider duck in a glass display case. She stared at that duck. She wondered if that was what a thousand years of island culture had been reduced to – some display panels and a stuffed duck. She didn't want this to be all she could show her children in the years to come. Anna could not accept this was the end. It sat wrong in her mind. It couldn't end like this.

The trouble was that the island needed more than what her father had been doing. Duck stations were disappearing. Now, only a few were left hanging on. There would only be a future for eider ducks on Måsøya if three things happened:

- Someone trapped the mink.
- Someone built the nests.
- Someone persuaded the ducks it was safe to come back.

Anna didn't know if this was possible. No one had ever brought ducks back to an island before. And she didn't have the time. Henning would have to stay home with the girls. And yet.

Our lives are a series of choices – about what we do, and don't do. Over time we decide what to let go of, what must die, and what we will fight to keep alive. Sometimes these are big, deliberate decisions, other times change happens in a thousand thoughtless little moments. Lying in her bed one night, the choice came to Anna, already made. The 'someone' who had to do that work was her. She knew it wouldn't be easy. There would be a price to pay – there always was when you changed things. But she did it anyway.

~

That second day had been slow. Showers rolled over the island and turned the well-trodden path to the outhouse to black mud and puddles. The fieldfares on the rocks behind the house were sodden. They shook their feathers from time to time. When the clouds broke, there were patches of blue sky. Ingrid went to see how much dried seaweed was stored in old laundry tubs and plastic buckets in the South Sea Barn, a gift to themselves from the season before, left each high summer on their final trip out. That stock of seaweed would be all we had to make nests with until we could dry some more.

Ingrid came back crestfallen. There was some, but it would soon run out. Anna didn't make it outside. Her batteries had gone flat. She told me to walk around the island, and, when I came back, she began to teach me the birds' names in Norwegian. I saw no ducks on the ocean.

Being on the island was affecting me more than I thought it would. I had always had a lot of control over my life and my days. But here I was, in their hands, working at their speed and as they saw fit. I was having to learn to be smaller and more malleable. This slow day by the fire, a day of listening, was quite unlike my normal life. The clock on the wall had stopped and no one cared. We were now governed by the rain, the clouds passing over, whatever the seabirds were doing, and the endlessly changing light. But above all it was the tides that dominated our waking hours. The island breathed beneath us, giant sighing breaths: in, and the water fell away, out, and the water rushed back.

~

That evening Anna asked if I would like a beer and came back with a can and a glass. She opened a packet of crisps for us to nibble at. Ingrid opened a bottle of wine. I felt deeply tired. And then it struck me that Anna had

92

changed her life when she was the age that I was now, the age – nearly fifty – when you wonder whether you have lived as well as you might, when you have to decide whether to stick or twist, carry on and accept your life, or strike out and make a change before it is too late.

I asked Anna about the moment when she'd told everyone what she wanted to do. The family bit had been easy, she said. Her girls were big enough to understand, and they knew her well enough to know that she loved being out on the islands. They were excited and wanted to help her. Henning had been supportive too. He could see she needed this.

But she couldn't go unless she got permission from her manager to take an extended period of leave. Not just for a one-off trip, but to go every spring. Anna suspected it would be a problem. She had never got on well with her boss, had grown to dread the sound of the woman's shoes click-clacking on the lino in the corridor as she came towards the kitchen. The woman was tall and blonde, with a mole on her nose, and had come from the mainland. She held herself upright like her backbone was made of cast iron. She would drive her fancy car to work, even though she lived a ten-minute walk away, just to park in the space reserved for the manager. She demanded shows of respect, which Anna had no intention of giving. She said either a place was run properly, or it was chaos. But Anna ran the kitchen her own way – if she wanted to make the old people biscuits, she did. In return, her boss had given her the worst shifts and the less well-paid overtime. For years, Anna had stubbornly refused to react. She'd never back down, bend, or pay lip service. But now, Anna needed something, and she had no option but to ask her boss for it.

Sure enough, it had been a disaster. Her boss had said she couldn't grant permission. The regulations didn't allow it. Anna was, technically, only working part-time, and had been since she had the children. It might have been possible if she'd worked full-time, but a part-time cook couldn't possibly take a month off work. 'But I'm taking it off unpaid,' Anna had blurted out. She could make it up to the home when she returned, and she had already taught the other girl in the kitchen how to cook everything, so they could manage in the meantime. Her boss was stony-faced. She offered to show Anna her employment contract and gestured to the filing cabinet.

The way Anna told this story made clear that it had been the fight of her life. The episode seemed to confirm her judgement on the modern world: they'd take everything you had and then make a slave of you.

Then she smiled and told me that hell would freeze over before she let that madam get the better of her. Word got round the home about what had happened. The other women said she could have their overtime, in order to qualify as full-time. And a few weeks later she marched back into her office and told her boss she was now eligible, and could she have permission. It was urgent. She needed to make ready for the coming ducks. Her boss stopped Anna talking, mid-flow, just by raising her hand. She told her she couldn't. She hadn't wanted to say so, but what was a middle-aged woman even thinking, going to live on the outermost islands, when she had a job and a family? These islanders were never happy unless their mouths were full of sea salt.

Here was the oldest of island clashes. On one side, the sensible, settled values of Vega and, on the other, an outer-island wildness that had never quite died.

~

Anna went home that night furious. Henning put the girls to bed and read their bedtime story, the *Folk Tales* by Asbjørnsen & Moe. She heard him doing silly voices for the trolls, the girls giggling. She wiped the kitchen table clean, then sat down and wrote a letter to the Norwegian government, to the department she'd read about in a recent newspaper as being responsible for the islands. The article had said that the government wanted to protect the old cultural traditions, but it was just talk. No one in government knew how to make a nest.

When he came downstairs, Henning read the letter in silence, then nodded, and Anna posted it the next morning. She felt better for having sent it, even if, as she suspected, there would be no reply.

In the days that followed, Anna daydreamed of quitting her job and going anyway, but she had no idea what work she would find afterwards, or how they'd pay their bills. They could probably manage, but she didn't really want to stop cooking for the old people. She didn't want a stranger keeping an eye on her father. She began to think she would have to settle for her life as it was.

A week later, she was called to her boss's office. She wouldn't look Anna in the eye. She said the mayor had been on the telephone. He'd been told by the government to ensure that a certain Anna Måsøy was to be released from her work for as long as was necessary to work on the abandoned duck station of Måsøyvær. She shuffled papers in a way that Anna had seen in movies, which seemed to mean this conversation was over and she should leave. Anna thought that her boss looked beaten, like a whipped dog, with her head down.

The mayor visited Anna in her home. He handed her a letter from the government and told her to keep it and show it to anyone that caused her trouble. She read the letter again and again. She took a copy to the old people's home in an envelope addressed to her boss, with a note telling her she would be gone from late April.

And that was how she had become a duck woman.

~

The stove was clicking with the heat, and we were all comfortable.

Breaking out of the old people's home was, I knew then, the defining moment of Anna's life. She had recognized that she had a choice: either to conform and be what everyone else wanted, or to step into the unknown and do what her heart said was right. She had dutifully constructed a normal life – a good one, with a marriage, a job, a family – but then, for reasons that didn't really make sense to anyone but her, she decided to leave it behind, to go back to something older, something she had only heard stories about. Hers was a tiny rebellion, hardly one to make the local newspaper, yet alone the history books, but it took courage, faith, and more than a little bit of defiance.

There was still a lot that didn't make sense to me. She hadn't answered my biggest question: what had happened to her family island? But in that moment, it didn't matter. I felt so proud I could have hugged her.

Anna seemed anything but proud. She waved her hand as if it was all nothing.

She slowly lifted herself out of her chair and creaked up the stairs to bed.

3.

Building

When I opened my eyes on the third morning everything felt different. The light flickering off the sea glowed round the edges of the rag of curtain. The seabirds to the north seemed noisier now that the wind had stopped. And there was a buzz around the kitchen. Ingrid was busy making breakfast. She seemed in a greater rush than normal. I went to get the salmon and ham and butter from the fridge in the porch, and laid them on the table. I asked Ingrid quietly whether the work could start now, and she nodded. She said we had to clear away the old seaweed nests, and air the huts and nest boxes, before we could begin remaking the nests. We would make more than three hundred nests, in perhaps a hundred woman-made structures, or 'huts'. I'd seen these scruffy, unoccupied buildings, boxes, and mounds scattered all across the island, ranging in size from a large suitcase to barns half as big as the house. I'd even spied the structures on little islets across the water, half a mile away. It sounded like a lot of work, and we were on a deadline: the ducks would be coming in from the open sea any day now. Anna still looked pale, sitting at the table, but she was smiling.

~

Over breakfast, Anna seemed to imply she would be working outside, but at the last moment, as Ingrid was putting on her outdoor clothes, she said apologetically, 'I must rest.' I wasn't sure I'd heard her correctly – we hadn't done much else so far but rest – but she must have said it, because she went back to her seat, and looked embarrassed. She could barely move.

The door clicked shut, and I found Ingrid had headed off to work without me. Her going alone hurt me a little. I wondered whether she was a bit fed up with me being there, taking her friend's talk away from her. Or perhaps she simply didn't think she could ask for my help, or, worse, that I would be of any use. Maybe she just thought the work fell entirely to her. But there was clearly far too much work for one old person, and I wasn't going to sit in the house for weeks doing nothing. I wondered for a moment whether I ought, out of politeness, only to observe their island life, staying in the shadows. But that seemed silly – I was able-bodied and strong, and Ingrid needed the help.

I found her across the windy headland, halfway into a duck hut. She looked surprised to see me. I said I was eating their food and had better earn my keep, so she should give me jobs to do, even if they only involved unskilled, dirty work. She looked sceptical but showed me how to clean away an old nest with a brisk explanation. I watched her for a moment more, opening hut doors and scraping away the mouldy or damp old nests, and then joined in. She corrected me when I did something wrong. Most of the seaweed was thrown out of the hut, but sometimes she would salvage some that was dry enough to be reused and leave it inside.

After a while I began to sense something was off. Ingrid was anxious. She kept looking back to the house, like she expected Anna to appear at any moment. After an hour or so, she said we had done enough. I was confused. We'd only cleared a few nests. There were hundreds more still to go. I wondered if I should offer to stay out and do the work, but realized that Ingrid could hardly allow me, a complete amateur, to rush at things. I followed her back to the house. We dawdled indoors for a while, then Ingrid seemed to find her courage again and we went back out and carried on working. Three times this happened. Ingrid appeared unsure how much to do without Anna's permission or approval.

~

That night, Anna said, 'You are very quiet.'

I told her I was fine, just adjusting to island life, and that she should not worry about me. But, in truth, I had not known how different life would be in such a place. There was no blaring TV, no internet, no social media, and even the radio was mostly turned off. There was no electricity until Anna started the generator every second or third day, so even our phones were used sparingly to save battery life. It was like revisiting the 1970s.

Ingrid barely spoke to me while we worked. The silence felt endless.

She said at least I was not alone like 'poor Marek'. A few years earlier, Lars had left a young Czech man called Marek on Fjærøy. He had been part of an international volunteer work programme. Lars had taken him out to the island to do carpentry on the barns. Then, for reasons known only to him, he left Marek working and went back to his farm on Vega. He told him not to worry, because Anna was coming the next day with food and firewood. But Lars hadn't checked, and Anna wasn't going for another week. She knew nothing about the stranger. When she arrived, she found the young man in a state. He'd slept on the floor by the stove, because it was bitterly cold. He had barely any food left and was confused about having been abandoned. Anna had brought him round with good food. But it had been a close call, she said, chuckling.

That night the women seemed uncomfortable, but unable to speak about what was bothering them. Ingrid seemed worried. It occurred to me that she must be hoping that Anna would come out to work soon because she was used to her being in charge.

~

The next day Ingrid and I went out again. Anna stayed on the sofa looking pale. We walked past the two little barns, down to the southern shore. Three snipe rose from the side of the path and zigged and zagged across the hillside. We got to two identical chicken huts – Storban 1 and Storban 2 – standing together like an upside-down W on the rock. They were about thirty feet above a little inlet. The water swilled in and out gently, lifting the kelp with each swell. The first hut had a door held in place by a rail that slotted in. Ingrid knocked it out and laid the door on the grass. I followed behind as she climbed into the shadows. She knelt between two wooden racks, which held scruffy old seaweed nests on either side of the hut, and indicated I should do what she did. She took off her gloves to feel the seaweed. I thought it looked dry, but she shook her head.

'If the seaweed is damp, soft, or mouldy, then it must go.'

She said the mother ducks were fussy about where they would lay their eggs. Using a rake-like tool she had brought with her, Ingrid clawed out the rubbish from the nesting racks. She gathered the debris from several nests, and pulled it out as she shuffled backwards, like a badger cleaning its sett. I copied her on the other side of the hut. My knees soon ached. The dried seaweed had broken down to a quartz-like black dust that covered the floor of the huts. As Ingrid cleaned, sooty clouds filled the sheds. She coughed and blew out her cheeks. We were both sweating. The dust stuck to our skin and made our faces dirty like coal miners. The debris was now piled outside the first hut, a tangled heap of old seaweed, some of it white and mouldy. We must leave the door open for a few days to let the sea wind take away the staleness, Ingrid said. The ducks liked these two huts, she explained, because they could waddle a few steps from their shadowed safety to the sea.

The second hut had a damp, rotten-fish, ammonia-like stink that curled our noses up. Otters had made it their home over winter. Ingrid pointed to the boulder by the exit, worn smooth with otter bellies and tails, where they had squeezed in and out under the timber. I grew up loving the book *Tarka the Otter*, so had no trouble imagining one sleeping through the howling gales, curled up in the old dry seaweed, under the noisy corrugated tin roof. I could see it in my mind, in the woodcut style of Charles Tunnicliffe. We cleaned away the nests and the refuse on the floor, but I could tell Ingrid's heart wasn't in it. She said, gloomily, 'The ducks will not come here with the smell of the otter.'

She asked me from time to time whether I thought the work was done right, and I shrugged. Then she'd look to the house for a reassurance that never came. We cleaned more nests, throwing the old seaweed down to the shore. After a while, a tiny, familiar figure appeared on the hillside. At last, Anna was coming to see us.

Ingrid told Anna about the otter smell. She agreed there was no way the ducks would nest there.

Anna seemed tired and uninterested in Ingrid's questions. She looked around, then trudged further up the hillside, towards the only tree on the island. I followed. There were two nest boxes by its trunk. She peered into one, then looked up at the tree. It was a sad, wind-twisted bird cherry tree, no taller than an old man, its branches reaching out like a clawed hand. It had grown out of a crack in the rock. The remnants of last year's carrion-crow nest were held in its tangled branches. Anna told me she had wanted to shoot the crow last year, but it was too clever. She looked at me and then nodded to the nest. I stood on the rocky shelf behind it, reached in, and pulled the brittle sticks apart and threw them across the hillside. If the crow had any sense, it would nest on another island.

We went back down to Ingrid, and I began helping her clean out some small nest boxes on the foreshore. When I looked up again, Anna had ghosted away without saying anything. We kept working round the huts, one by one, past the sea barn and along the grassy shore. One hut had lost its wooden peg catch, so Ingrid hammered on a new one. She said her husband, a carpenter, would despair at her lack of skill. After a while I offered to help. I'd grown up using a hammer and saw but hadn't been sure how to offer without patronizing her.

When we got back to the house, later, Anna was staring out the window. I felt unbearably sad for her. She looked finished. Ingrid made broth and ladled it into bowls. The bits of carrot, turnip, potato, and ham glowed as I sipped it from my spoon. We had crunchy flatbreads with it, thick with butter.

~

The pace of the work was slow. I had to remind myself that, though Ingrid was strong, she was well into her sixties. Twenty or more years older than me. She seemed to have a numerical target in her head for how many huts we had to clean out each day. The whole project relied upon constructing nests for any and every duck that came ashore, to allow them to sit, lay, and incubate their eggs. This had to happen by the time the ducks decided to come ashore, but we continued at this frustratingly slow pace.

We would often do an hour of work and then go back to the house for a coffee. The days were made up of many little bursts of cleaning and airing.

Open the door.

Drag out the old damp and mouldy nests.

Leave the door open.

Repeat.

Hundreds of times.

Until the point each afternoon when she would say we had done enough.

The early days were grey, but the rain stayed away. We plodded on with the work, but Ingrid seemed anxious. Anna stayed by the fire. The whole island felt strange because she was not outside.

It was like being at Troy but with Achilles unwell, in his tent, and the other soldiers lost without him. Anna not leading the work created a vacuum that neither Ingrid nor I wanted to, or knew how to, fill.

I tried to be as loyal to Ingrid as she was to Anna, a

foot soldier who could help get the nests cleaned. Gradually, we found a rhythm working in tandem up either side of the huts, or leapfrogging each other from nest box to nest box until whole sections of the foreshore were done. Ingrid nodded encouragement when I went to the next hut. One day we managed to clean out some fifty nests. Back at the house, Ingrid made fishcakes and boiled potatoes, and told Anna I could work hard.

~

There is no learning quite so good as doing. Cleaning the nests with Ingrid, I became familiar with all the places the ducks would nest in. We knelt on the floor of wooden huts that looked like garden sheds, or repurposed chicken huts. We reached into boxes that held two or three nests, made from fishing trays, and recycled wooden fish boxes that held just one. We leaned into the stalls in the cow byres. And shuffled on our bellies into the spaces beneath the house and the barns.

Each nest site had a name written on the front in flaking old black paint. Being able to locate the action would become vital in the nesting time. Within a month I would be speaking of duck happenings in Naustban and Sørodden, Misjonshuset, Ban på håjen, or Trondsen, as if they were places I had known my whole life.

~

Nothing about those early days on the island was quite what I had imagined. I had come to this, the wildest of places, to learn from Anna. The sense she had given me when I first met her was that it was possible to step outside history. She had seemed untouchable. Unbreakable. I couldn't wait to see her in action. But with each passing day, it started to look like Anna might be defeated – like this was a season too far. I worried I'd come too late.

Instead of being apprenticed to Anna, I was working with another woman entirely. I felt for her. Ingrid had come to help her friend, not do all the work herself and be lumbered with a stranger. Occasionally I felt a weary emptiness and wondered why I was not with my family at home, on my own farm.

And I began to worry. What if Anna didn't get stronger? What if she got worse and had to leave the island? What if the weather was bad and a boat couldn't come? I was grateful for Ingrid's presence; I had no idea how to handle an emergency on the island, if one should come to pass. It was like someone had pressed pause on Anna – she was there enough to chat to us at mealtimes or in the evenings, but she couldn't work, and she wasn't emitting her customary powerful aura. The woman on the sofa was a tired seventy-year-old with high blood pressure.

I began to see that Ingrid was far more capable than she thought she was. She knew more about the work than she said she did, and she cared so much about it that, despite her doubts, it was done well. Her reports in the house, several times a day, made Anna visibly uncomfortable.

She seemed almost ashamed to be indoors whilst Ingrid worked so hard. And she didn't want to talk about it, so the gaps between reports grew longer.

I think Anna knew she was being a little cold with Ingrid. It must have been hard for this strong island woman, who had always got things done, now her body was refusing to comply. Her face was puffy, and her skin waxy. Everything seemed an effort. Her days were filled only with knitting, half-hearted bursts of housework, and our coffee breaks. One day she brushed the dust to a corner of the brown and orange linoleum floor, and took the sheepskin rugs from the backs of the chairs and whacked them gently on the end of the barn to get the dust out. But, mostly, she sat wrapped in a thick grey woollen throw, one eye always on the sea beyond the glass.

~

For the first week or two on the island, we never saw a duck. Anna said this was quite normal. The eiders were still out at sea, where they lived their whole lives, except for the few weeks when they came to the islands. She had seen a couple of pairs on the journey out. They were on the deeper open water of the fjord, between Vega and the down islands. I'd seen a lone male flash past the boat, a winged blur of cream and green, flying low over the waves. Anna said that most of their lives on the ocean were spent in groups, sometimes in rafts thousands of ducks strong. They had frenzied bursts of feeding when they dived for shellfish, crabs and starfish on the ocean floor. Once they had eaten, they rested and digested and groomed their plumage, bobbing on the waves.

If it weren't for the fact that everything tried to eat them, Anna said, the shallow sea around Fjærøyvær would be a paradise for eider ducks.

~

One afternoon, we were standing on the decking by the house. Anna became very still, and stared down to the incoming tide. The seaweed was lifting on the rising water. I tried to see what she was looking at. She whispered that something dark, like a mink, had moved in the distance. Later I saw that she had lifted the rifle out of the porch from behind the jackets, its bullets laid on the worktop. Anna told me to walk the perimeter of the island, and to take the gun. She wanted the wild things, not least mink, otters, and ravens, to be fearful, because that was a precondition for nesting ducks. Being there and watching was a significant part of the work, for Anna. She was the island's eyes.

We do not think of watching the world around us as work. Work is usually muscular and rushed at – but that was a misplaced way of thinking on the island. Even on the busiest days of the season that followed, there were always quiet hours when Anna simply watched. She drew no distinction between looking out the window and physically doing jobs – they were one and the same.

Anna was not strong enough to do rough outside work, but, as the days passed, she grew more and more interested in about what we had seen and done.

The talk in the little white house was mostly of wild things – the raven searching for nests across the bay, the mink Ingrid thought she had seen, or the golden eagle that passed high above as we worked. Anna said that both kinds of eagles – golden and sea eagles – lived on the coast, but she mostly saw sea eagles. I had two small boys and I knew that they would ask me which eagle would win in a fight. Anna said a fisherman she knew had once seen a golden eagle get too close to a sea eagle in the sky above his boat. The sea eagle had grabbed it, crumpled it in a fistful of talons, and tossed it, like trash, down to the waves.

Anna started to cook and look after us better when we came back in. She served us folded flatbreads – soft, pancake-like things layered with butter, sugar, and cinnamon – which she called *lefse*. And one afternoon she started the generator to bake bread in the oven. Hard, brown wholemeal bread, already half-baked from the Spar. The generator purred under its hinged roof by the pantry while we had our dinner. Carly Simon's 'You're So Vain' filled the room.

~

For a week or so we had not told many stories. Ingrid and I had thrown ourselves into the clearing and cleaning.

I could not believe that Anna would spend the whole of her last season just watching from the house. Somehow, I felt sure that she would overcome this setback and be back outside before long. I said as much to her one night. She laughed, and said that she was older now, and, besides, the inside work mattered, too.

She told me about the first time she'd come to Fjærøyvær, which belonged to an old man on Vega called Terje. I'd heard his name once or twice before but hadn't deciphered who he was. She said the house had been a wreck when she first arrived. She had focused her efforts on the kitchen and the modest living room. The ceiling in the living room had been black with mould and dirt. She had scrubbed and scrubbed it till her hands ached. Three times she'd had to paint it with white emulsion, before it stopped looking grubby. She'd brought the paint from home in half-used tins, and found brushes in Terje's workshop, a crammed tool shed made of plywood planks that took up half the space of the ground floor. She cleaned the glass and painted the window frames. She did her repairs without spending money, because she didn't have any and it wasn't her house. She had lifted Terje's pictures carefully from the walls so she could paint. There were old sepia photographs of favourite sheep and scraggy island cows, ships on fjords on brilliant blue days, small paintings of waterfalls tumbling in forest glades, and frozen winter scenes. In one picture, a man was mauled by a polar bear, his mate levelling a rifle to kill it. In another, a faithful dog was hugged by children in bedtime smocks. She'd lifted a portrait of the last Queen of Norway and put it safely to one side.

She pointed to the wall by the door. There was a pencil sketch of a woman. Her wavy brown hair was tied up in a bob, and she had a long, elegant nose, and seductive blue eyes. She was wearing a fashionable yellow blouse from, perhaps, the 1920s. Anna explained she had found the picture under a bed when she was cleaning the house. The glass in the frame was broken. She believed the woman was what was called a *hulder*. I'd understood that a *huldra* was a kind of female troll that lived beneath the ground. This sketch was of someone pretty, so I thought she was joking. When a smile formed on my face, I sensed Anna's irritation. So I asked, more respectfully, about the *huldra*, explaining that in England no one believed in such things. Anna told me the *huldra* had been seen many times on this island.

So many times, in fact, that the women on Vega had told her not to take the job here. The people on Flatholm claimed to have seen a giant woman on the island from their fishing boats. And, when the woman had turned to hide from them, they'd seen the swish of a tail. Anna told me that *huldra* were famous for playing tricks on humans, particularly men. They tangled fishing lines, hid tools, and caused accidents. The duck woman before Anna had said she'd seen the *huldra*, too. She would always leave one stall empty in the cow byre, so the trolls could feed and milk their cow when no one was around. *Huldra* cows, Anna said, were blue.

Huldra in many tales were fearsome, but Anna had her own take on them. They lived shadow lives to us humans. Mostly, they went unseen, but occasionally people caught glimpses of them. Her grandmother had told her stories about seeing a *huldra* on Måsøy. She hadn't been scared, and nor was Anna.

She said that the first season she'd spent here, the *huldra* had helped her. Anna had worked tirelessly for weeks, building and mending huts and nests. She had scavenged what timber she could from the shoreline, and dragged lengths of corrugated tin across the rocks and sawn them into squares for new roofs. She had built more and more nests. And when Terje came to the island to see her progress, he was delighted with her work. The duck station had been transformed.

Then, just before the ducks came in to nest, there was a terrible storm. Anna had heard on the radio that it was approaching and had tied everything down with ropes and stones. She banked up the fire and hunkered down in the little white house under some blankets. That night the winds howled around her, every joint and joist in the house seemed to heave and strain and creak, and she feared the roof might rip off. She had tried to call home, but her phone wouldn't work. The storm raged on. She couldn't sleep. When she dared look out the window in the darkness, she got glimpses through the rain of huge, Hokusai-like waves cresting all around, drowning everything except the highest rocks, and racing on to the mainland. She feared the houses on Flatholm would be smashed to kindling. Thuds and bumps could be heard out in the darkness. All night those giant waves roared and crashed.

Eventually, she fell asleep, and when she woke all was still and quiet. A strange light shone through the windows. She looked out and gasped. This was what the world must have looked when Noah and his family saw the land reappear from beneath the flood. She went out and there was flotsam and jetsam everywhere. Roof tiles blown off. Giant drifts of seaweed spewed up on the headlands. The rocks were scoured clean. And her work was smashed to pieces. The stone and wooden nest boxes on the lowest headlands were all gone.

It was a disaster. She had almost no time before the ducks were due to arrive, and no money to replace the materials she had lost. She had to find and retrieve whatever she could. She looked through her binoculars and could see some of her wooden nest boxes on the rocks, half a mile away, swept over the bay and tossed up onto the western edges of Flatholm. She rowed out across the spent sea to the islands. Birds were screeching, a feeding frenzy taking place in the rock pools. As she pulled her nest boxes, or bits of them, out of the tangles of seaweed, she could see the houses on Flathom were all still standing. She was surprised to find some of her wooden boxes set neatly on the rocks, like they'd been gently placed there. It was as though someone had helped her while she'd been asleep. The *huldra* must have pulled them up out of the water. She rowed around the headlands and skerries salvaging what she had lost, and more. The waves had washed up amazing amounts of good timber and other material she could use. She went home with the boat fully loaded.

She remembered her grandmother's eyes sparking wild when she told tales about storms. Violent weather had always brought blessings as well as tragedies. The islanders had long benefited from scavenging anything of value from ships that wrecked on the rocks. Their houses were sometimes built from timbers taken from wrecks, and ornate carvings from their bows still sometimes adorned their walls. Anna harvested the aftermath of that storm to build again. The storm was a test, and Anna had passed.

~

As the days passed, and more and more nests were cleared, Ingrid looked to the house less and less. She grew more comfortable using me as a labourer. I even got an occasional smile out of her. I did the fetching and carrying, and the rougher work. There was not much beauty in those grey early days. And we were not the only ones on the island. One afternoon, I nearly jumped out of my skin when I saw a shuffle in the grass, and a flash of brown hair, an indistinct blob, hurrying away. Ingrid chuckled and said it was a 'land rat', like a big fat mole the size of a shoe. These island colonizers were locked in a perpetual cycle of boom and bust, feast and famine. By the end of winter, they'd nibbled the turf bare and ploughed the soil with strange tunnels half-open to the sky. We'd sometimes watch the short-eared owl hunting them on South Island. When the land rats got hungry, Ingrid said, they swam away to find new islands to colonize. Fishermen saw them on the move, masses of little, brown rattish heads poking out of the waves.

Then the weather broke. The rain poured down our necks, and our hands howled with the cold. The rowing boat needed the rainwater bailed out, to stop it sinking. Ingrid was stressed: she had planned to dry the seaweed, but now it lay sodden where it had been thrown.

Nest cleaning in the rain was a dour business. Pathways filled with puddles, then became streams. The thin island soil was soon waterlogged and muddy. Oystercatchers piped and chased each other across the black shore. Sometimes we chatted and told each other stories about our lives. Other times I felt unbearably lonely and homesick. When we got back to the house, we had smudged, wet knees. We'd try to wash our blackened hands with cold water and soap. I learnt to pull my socks over my trouser bottoms to stop the earwigs that would nip and leave welts on my legs.

The rain slowed our work. Anna being so weak made it all feel like a denial of reality. It was hard to stay upbeat when we were tired and we kept going only by loyalty to Anna. Ingrid told me her husband could come and help, but she knew Anna would see that as a betrayal.

~

Watching Anna fail was a humbling experience. It was, I began to see, a foreshadowing of what lay ahead for me. You had to be young and in good health to fight the world. In her prime, Anna had been so hell-bent on recreating the golden age of her family that she had never faltered. She had done it alone. She'd endured seasons when the weather was sour and nasty. Days when she couldn't open the front door because it was held firm by the wind. Nights when her friends rang her and asked if she was OK, and she gritted her teeth and said yes.

Though she seemed like a fading lamp, every now and then she'd flicker a little, say something wicked or wilful, and I'd see a glint in her eyes again. There was just enough character in those glances for me to keep faith: this wasn't over yet.

~

The days passed. The grass and clumps of water marigolds slowly greened around the house. Eventually Ingrid and I finished cleaning and airing the nests on the main island and the neighbouring islets that we could walk to at low tide. There was still more of this work to do on the islands further out, but, one morning, we woke to a drying wind. The clouds were high in the sky now, and the light had changed. At breakfast, Anna looked different. She sounded more cheerful. She told Ingrid that she appreciated all of her hard work. Ingrid said she was glad of my help and nodded to me. It was time to turn the seaweed, Anna said. Ingrid smiled at me.

We put on our wellington boots and the three of us walked down the path together. The sun was warm on our faces. We took long-handled hay forks from the log shed and headed towards Crow Island. We crossed a little stone causeway made of boulders and topped with turf, which spanned a sunken fault-line that was slowly being gouged out by storms, about six feet wide. The ravine was littered with rusty old sheets of corrugated iron and timbers thrown there to rot. Ingrid led the way. She stepped down the slope to where the sea had been an hour before. She carefully crossed the slippery rocks. Anna stood and watched us wistfully. She could not follow, whatever she had hoped. The rocks were too rough and slimy. She decided to inspect the nest huts on the hillside instead. Her fork was left leaning on a duck hut.

Crow Island was, at low tide, only a few metres away from the main island, but when the tide came in, it might as well have been half a mile away. Now the tide was out and we could walk through a gully that had until an hour ago been part of the ocean bed. This sister island was quite different in character: a rounded lump of granite almost swept over by the biggest winter waves, emerging again in calmer sea like a whale's back. There was no topsoil and no grass, only juniper and small alpine plants growing between the rocks. The far side was the north-ern boundary of our sea estate, where it met a deep and fast-flowing tidal channel. A snow bunting cheeped from the top of a triangular duck hut, then flitted about the foreshore from rock to rock, chasing its mate. The shoreline was littered with wooden debris thrown up by the sea. Old tree stumps, beams from broken shipwrecks and lengths of 2x4. The island had a collection of nests – two triangular huts, a few nest boxes, and half a dozen old stone nests. But we weren't here for the nests, not yet: we had come to dry the seaweed. This was a perfect place for the job, because its big, flattish slabs of rock were exposed to the sun and wind. If we could get it dry enough, it would be used to make the nests throughout the sea estate.

The seaweed had been thrown up on to the drying-rocks for us. It made me think about the *huldra*, invisible folk, helping us. But Ingrid explained that Anna's daughters, who now lived in Oslo, had visited their mother on Vega a couple of weeks earlier. They'd been out here, briefly, and had thrown forkfuls of damp seaweed on to the rocks to begin drying. They'd tossed it further and further up to the most exposed rocks, where the sun and wind could now do its work, above the high-tide mark. They'd prepared this for us. We stepped across the fissures in the rocks to get up to this drying place, where the seaweed lay waiting, like hay in fresh-mown rows.

Our fork prongs soon chimed, ting, ting, ting, as they caught the rocks – a gentle, rhythmic sound as we worked. The seaweed was silver and black like charcoal where it had dried out, and still damp green below. Ingrid used one prong of her fork to skilfully pick under the edge of a clump and peeled it from the rock where it had dried like a scab. It held to the rock a little at first, then broke free. She flicked it up and over, and let it fall back stiffly to the ground. She lifted forkful after forkful and spread it evenly. We had to turn it until it was thoroughly dry. I had grown up handling two-pronged hay forks, so I knew this work. Ingrid seemed surprised. I told her some things were familiar here, and others strange. I had never made hay on a rock far out at sea. I went to the most jagged rocks, where the seaweed was already dry. The tangles and bubbles made each forkful look like the matted hair of a drowned witch.

The seaweed smelled more like the sea than the sea itself. Soon it was all turned. Ingrid walked up one of the cracks in the rock and found the remnants of a stone hut, just above the high tide mark, and set about rebuilding it. She glanced to where Anna had been, but there was no one in sight. She returned to her work, perhaps with a little more confidence, knowing it would not be checked.

~

We'd been on the island for more than a week now. When Ingrid saw I was taking Anna's work seriously – as seriously as she did – and respecting her guidance, she warmed to me. Our conversation was moving beyond basic instructions. As we dried seaweed and rebuilt huts together, she began to tell me more about her life. Her earlier coldness melted like a glacier in the sun.

~

Ingrid had worked in the bank on Vega for forty-two years. She would drive to town each morning from her house at the northenmost end of the island – down the gravel road and through the forest. Her feet crunched across the gravel in the car park in summer, and through the snow and ice in winter. She opened the doors and turned on the lights and the computers. She chatted with the older folk when they came to bank their pensions. She helped farmers and fishermen put money in their savings or get loans to buy fields or tractors and boats. She knew everyone by name, and knew things about their finances that would have surprised the local gossips – but she never spoke a word of anyone's business outside the bank. It wasn't exactly exciting work, but real life often isn't. It helped her and her husband pay the bills and bring up their family. But towards the end, she told me, she'd lost heart in it. They sent some young man in a suit from Oslo to the bank. He had fancy corporate ideas about how they needed to sell 'products', like insurance, to 'customers'. He returned south, and she felt uneasy about it all. The customers were her friends and fellow islanders. They didn't want the stuff she was supposed to sell them. She didn't want to make money from them. If she had to choose between the island people and the bank, she knew where her loyalties lay. She couldn't wait to go home each night.

Her husband, Stig, had built their house. He'd made her a room for weaving, and even constructed her a wooden loom. The kitchen looked over the sea. Stig was often out there fishing in his wooden boat. She would help her daughter with her homework, or be cooking the supper, with the CB two-way radio on. Through the static, she'd hear the fishermen talking about where to find the fish. It was good to know that Stig was safe. By coincidence, the duck women on the islands used the same radio frequency. Ingrid was intrigued by these women working far out on the grey rocks she gazed at as she washed the dishes. They unsettled her. They fell outside the rules she lived her own life by. Slowly, she realized that she envied them. Their talk was full of the ocean. They told each other what the ducks were doing, and where mink or otter had been seen, and relayed orders back to the Spar for groceries. They took no shit and would tongue-lash the fishermen for getting too close to the duck islands. The men would bluster back at them but would do as they were told. The farmers on Vega tended to dismiss these women – said they should have been home making supper, not messing about with ducks. But Ingrid was fascinated by them. Her grandmother had been a duck woman, and Ingrid had gone out to visit her regularly as a girl. But by the time she was a teenager it was only a memory. Island work had faded out of her life. She had got on with school, then work;

she'd married and had a daughter. She did all the stuff she had to do. But, every July, a woman came into the bank with calloused hands and sunburnt cheeks, and an other-worldly air, like she didn't give a damn what anyone else thought, or about the bills she now had to pay, or what was happening with the school PTA. The woman was Anna.

The combination of remembering her grandmother and seeing Anna nagged at her – it said something else was possible. One autumn, she offered to help Anna clean the eiderdown she'd brought back to Vega. It was like working with her grandmother again. They spent hours with the radio on, cleaning eiderdown between their knees. Ingrid loved the sense of calm that came with the work. Then, she started going out to the island with her for a few days at a time, to help. She began to wonder about retiring from the bank. Her daughter was grown up and married, and had moved to the mainland. Ingrid had done many years of sensible and was ready to do what she wanted for a change.

~

Then Ingrid found a lump in her breast. She had chemo-therapy and was very poorly – it wasn't clear she would make it through. She lost her hair and thought it was probably the end. It made her wonder a lot about her life, and what she might have done if she had had more time. Thankfully, with the treatment the cancer went into remission, and, as she got a bit of strength back, she went to help Anna in the barn again.

One day, over coffee, Anna surprised her. She said she needed someone to go with her to the duck station for the whole season. The authorities had told Anna that it wasn't safe for a woman to be out there alone, and she must have a partner. Health and safety. Anna thought this was nonsense but had to comply. She had feared Ingrid was too ill for the task, but there was no one else Anna wanted with her. And she sensed the island-longing in her friend.

Stig agreed. He would manage fine at home and would come and see her when he could. If she got worse, he would fetch her home and nurse her. It was all much easier than Ingrid had thought.

Anna looked after her on the island. She cooked her simple broths and lots of fish and potatoes. They talked for hours about their children and their lives. Ingrid was in a bad way, much worse than she had let on to Stig. Her knuckles were so swollen she soaked her hands in the salty rock pools. But she loved being there. It was different staying for an extended length of time – she was able to tune in to it all. And the world became spellbindingly beautiful when you thought you were dying.

As the weeks passed, Ingrid became stronger. Her flaxen hair grew back, and thicker than ever. Her pale, blotchy skin became brown and healthy. She ate like a horse, and Anna teased her that she was getting her 'sexy' shape back. When she returned home at the end of the season, a friend passed her in the supermarket aisle and didn't recognize her. The woman had hugged her, touched her hair, felt her muscles, and kissed her cheeks – as if Ingrid had crawled back from the dead.

'You look amazing,' she had said.

Ingrid had replied, 'The island was my medicine.'

Now, Ingrid said, we needed the island to mend Anna.

~

The headlands all around the island were soon a patchwork of drying-fields. A sea crop turned each day or so, every field a different shade of grey. As we ate our supper, night after night, the women nervously discussed whether we had dried enough for the nests. Each night they agreed that we hadn't. On the fourth drying day, Anna said, 'I think we have enough now.'

~

I was happier now that we were busy. Working gave the days purpose and stopped me feeling like a stranger. The coming of the ducks had loomed over us since we'd arrived on the island nearly a fortnight ago, and the more I understood about the work, the more anxious I became about getting it done in time. If I asked the women when the ducks might come, they'd only shrug. I guessed, from one of their discussions, it was maybe ten days away. There was a mountain of work to do in preparation. All we had done so far was air the huts and dry the seaweed. Now we had to use the dried seaweed to make nests in every single structure across all the islands and islets.

Each day Anna came out for a little longer and did a little more. She took me to clear out the nests sheltered under an old wooden rowing boat called *Ester*. The upside-down boat was propped up at a 45-degree angle by a low wall of wooden rails and corrugated tin, and in that wall was a door-hatch that could be removed. Once inside, the hand-carved beams and ribs of the old boat arced over me like a cathedral roof. Anna stayed on the outside and instructed me with her head poking through the door.

Every nesting place had a story. Next to *Ester* was an old fibreglass boat-cabin with mouldy green windows. A sheet of half-rotten plywood held up by a length of iron pipe served as the door. The cabin had been left behind by a fisherman named Odd, Anna explained, and they'd named this spot after him.

She told me the ducks were afraid of anything new, and had strong opinions about where they would and would not nest each spring. They were fussy. Some liked the stone huts, some chose the barns, some liked to be tucked away under the house. Eiders live longer than most ducks – around twenty years – and they were faithful to their chosen homes on the island, coming back to these nooks and crannies year after year. She speculated that perhaps their own mothers had hatched them in these very same places. Their whims and choices filled Anna's brain, she was endlessly fascinated by them. Her stories from this time often went unfinished – she would walk away to the next job, or to look at something important along the headland. Then she would vanish, and Ingrid and I would go back to working together. We would sit on the grass or the rocks catching our breath. I felt accepted now, part of something, not just an observer. These two women were so genuine and earnest, and resolute in their belief that the work mattered, that I found myself swept along with them.

Back home, everyone looked to me for the rebellion and the spirit, and over time that had sickened me of it. That's why, I remembered, geese take turns at the front when they migrate, because the front bird is working the hardest, and the others ride in its slipstream. So, rather sensibly, they drop back after a while, to catch their breath, and are pulled along while they recover. Men are not so wise. I felt like I had been the front goose for too long. Worn myself out. But here I could simply be one of the foot-soldiers and do basic, practical things with Anna and Ingrid, to help the birds.

One day, on a break, I dared to ask Ingrid if she had originally thought my coming to the island was a bad idea. She laughed and said, 'Yes! A terrible idea.' But now she wasn't sure how the work would have got done without me. She was relieved I was there. I saw Anna smile, as if to say, 'I told you so.'

They began to give me bigger servings, like it was a

good investment. Bowls of porridge with cinnamon. Cod and white sauce. Platefuls of bacon and egg. One night we had sago pudding and blackcurrant jam. Afterwards, they both sat smiling at me as they knitted.

Anna asked if there were any other spare Englishmen available for island work, and could I call them. The pay was board and lodgings.

~

When the huts had all been cleaned, mended, and aired, and the seaweed was dry, it was time for nest-making. I was tempted to turn the calendar on the kitchen wall to May, but noticed that it had been hung years ago. Time was losing its old meaning.

The first day of nest-making, Ingrid took me to Crow Island and we packed armfuls of the now-brittle seaweed into square canvas shopping bags and washing tubs. After an hour my arms ached. The bags were not heavy but were clumsy to haul across the slippy rocks. Ingrid trod tentatively across the rocks and through the gullies, putting a hand down to steady herself. For larger loads we'd heap up the wheelbarrow – which I thought I heard Ingrid call the 'land-boat' – with bags and then wobble down the island paths, getting as close as we could to where it was next needed. Anna could not yet do the rougher work but was now marshalling our efforts. She had a natural authority. She never raised her voice, always spoke quietly, and yet Ingrid and I hung on her words – she simply knew more about everything here than we did. And she now seemed deeply grateful for our work. She saw the sweat on Ingrid's forehead and told her to stop and rest. We drank black coffee from fine, Dresden blue-and-white patterned teacups and they asked me what food I loved, so they could make it.

~

Anna showed me how to make a nest. Watching her work was like watching a master craftsman – her hands were practised and clever and fast. She seemed determined to set the standard and make sure I did this work right. Each nest was an act of love.

She crawled on her belly under the barns, or shuffled in on her knees, or crouched low into the huts, to make them. She dragged armfuls of dry seaweed in with her. A pile of older, matted seaweed, some of which we'd rescued and recycled from the previous year, was used as a base layer. Sometimes a sheet of plywood was added beneath that, if the nest was on damp ground, or if the previous year there had been feather mites there. Then she pulled a small armful of springy, dry seaweed from a bag or plastic tub, and laid it in a rough circular shape, like making a Christmas wreath out of brittle branches. As Anna turned this nest shape, she pushed it inwards from the sides, and patted it down strongly so the seaweed bound itself in place. The dried seaweed was coarse and stubborn, so each scruffy nest was patted, pushed, and crunched into something that was round and heaped. She wore rubber gloves and made me do the same, but the seaweed was spiky and still made our hands sore. Making the nests, I sometimes thought of the crown of thorns that Jesus wore on the cross. Some-one must have bound that crown round and into itself, like we were doing now – although the seaweed was only prickly, not thorned. Anna's final touch was a crunchy layer of small broken seaweed flakes in the middle of the nest; the duck would nestle down here to make her laying bed. Anna topped up her supply of fine shards by grinding down the brittle-dry seaweed using the top of a claw hammer and a small blue petrol drum, like a pestle and mortar. Though I'd been taught how to make the nests, Anna's focus on perfection made me nervous about trying. Instead, I brought her the materials she needed. And bashed down the seaweed and broke it into smaller stuff, until my hands were swollen. By night, we were all worn out and grumbling about our backs. Anna could barely move from the sofa, but she was cheerful. Each night she listed in her diary the number of nests we had made.

Anna told me she loved making the nests, and I could see now that she had been saving herself for this. She sent me to work in the less vital places, using her energy on the busiest and more valuable huts and nest boxes. She was obsessive about those ones being done right. She fussed and fiddled over their shape and depth, because the ducks were incredibly fussy too. This obsessive level of care was, I now saw, the difference between a good duck woman and an amateur. I was an amateur, but it didn't matter. I felt a surge of happiness and relief that this woman I so admired was back in her element. She oozed purpose, and Ingrid and I fed off it, rushing here and there helping and doing whatever she needed. I felt foolish for ever having thought that this woman with her iron will could be finished.

After two or three days of nest-making, Anna sent Ingrid and me to work on the nests on Crow Island, which was still out of reach for her. When I made nests, Ingrid gave them a little prod or pat, or added a little bit of seaweed, and then nodded. We did our best together. We were soon tired, so we sat in the sunshine and looked out across the tidal zone. I felt a surge of awe at the beauty of this place. I ran and stood on a giant rock, held my arms out wide, and said, 'Ingrid, let's get married and live here forever.'

She laughed so hard she nearly fell off her rock. She couldn't wait to tell Anna. And that night, in the house, they kept giggling about it as we drank our wine.

~

The next morning, we were all working in one of the duck huts by the house when a boat came round the headland, its engine echoing across the bay. Ingrid set down her washing basket of seaweed and headed down the path.

Anna, on her knees, carried on working. She crunched seaweed into the shape of a nest, almost punching it down with her gloved fists. She seemed irritated. I heard two men's voices down by the bay, ropes being pulled and tied, heavy steps on the planks, and the sound of boxes being tossed on to the wooden wharf.

The boat was Ingrid's husband's. It seemed to me that Ingrid hadn't been entirely surprised by his arrival. She hadn't looked Anna in the eye when she got up. Anna clearly thought this was a stitch-up. Ingrid had been openly worrying about whether we would get the work done in time. I felt a little sorry for her. I could hardly blame her if she had called her husband a few days earlier, when things were looking bleak, and I could hardly blame him for coming to help. The trouble was, Anna was now back at work. 'This is still my duck station,' she said to me, getting slowly to her feet. She stood and watched as Ingrid and her husband chatted in the distance. He had another man with him. Anna told me the men would pretend they were just passing by.

The visitors soon broke the spell of the place, crowded it with noise. If she was too welcoming, Anna said, people would never stop coming and some would never leave. Someone on Vega would say that such-and-such a person had been out to Fjærøyvær, the tale would grow in the telling, and then Terje would call her and complain that she was running a holiday resort on his island. Part of her job was keeping people away. It was good that folk feared the tongue of a duck woman. But people quickly took liberties when they saw someone fading and losing strength.

And now it was complicated.

There were certain things the two women never spoke about. Chief among these was what would happen on the island after Anna's day. Ingrid avoided the topic out of respect and deference. Anna, because it was painful. Both of them knew that, ultimately, it wasn't their decision, but the owner's.

Stig was less deferential. Anna sensed he wanted to get here and get on with things in his own way with his wife.

~

Stig came up the path with his friend following behind. He said they were just passing on their way home from fishing. They thought they might as well call in to say hello and had brought us some of their catch. Stig walked past Anna to the house. Anna looked to me and breathed in deeply. She said the ducks had not yet come, so it could have been worse. We followed after him. A few minutes later they were all seated on chairs on the decking at the end of the white house, chatting and laughing in the sunshine like teenage friends. Anna seemed to have swallowed her annoyance. There was no point to it now. They drank black coffee and ate the cake and brown cheese Ingrid carried through from the kitchen. The men had gossip from home, little of which I could understand. They said they had brought good fish, caught from a little bay beyond the islands. Ingrid clapped her hands gently and said she would make fried fish in butter for supper.

They told Anna about the birds they had seen at sea. Hundreds of barnacle geese had flown over their boat in the mist, chattering like they were lost and asking the way to Svalbard. Stig showed her blurry photos from his phone, and one was of a mink they had killed on a skerry, being held up by its tail. Anna smiled at the photo. She hated mink.

Stig asked for the fish knives, and Anna went to get them. He took the knives, toyed with them in his hands, feeling their edges with his gnarled fingers, and laughed with his friend at how blunt they were. Women can't sharpen knives, he said to me. His friend laughed, but I didn't. Stig said the barn needed repairs, and some of the duck huts were ramshackle. I couldn't tell if he was offering to help or criticizing. Either way, Anna looked like thunder. He wasn't the boss of what needed doing here.

Ingrid poured them a glass of liquor each. Stig downed his and wiped his grey whiskery face with the back of his sleeve. They told stories about when they were young, and had another drink, and then another. Time passed and the two men grew louder – half-drunk boys in old men's bodies. Anna had withdrawn from the conversation and seemed to be waiting for the men to shut up and go. The men sensed I wasn't on their team and gave up trying to chat to me.

Ingrid looked torn between her best friend and her husband. Anna's stubborn silence slowly unsettled the men, and made them play up a little more, talking even louder.

Then Stig sensed something had changed. He said to his friend that they'd better get some jobs done. He sat and sharpened all of the house knives on a blue stone. His friend mended the nest boxes by the barn with a hammer and some nails.

Anna seemed to calm down again. She looked admiringly at Stig's skill with the sharpening stone, and made him another coffee. Later she'd tell me that Stig was a craftsman, a retired house builder, and he did everything with care.

After supper the men said their goodbyes and left. The boat was hardly out of the bay before Anna became her old self once more. She never mentioned them again. Soon it was like they had never come, as if her irritation had blown away on the wind.

~

The next week went by in a blur of nest-making. It was simple, repetitive work and I began to lose myself in it. This was Anna's world, and, once I tuned in to her cares and her jobs, there was a plainness to it that I loved. It was settling and calming being beside her and Ingrid.

There was a togetherness too, now – the kind that comes from working side by side for many hours on the same tasks. And satisfying because everywhere we went we left beautiful, hand-crafted nests behind us.

We saw so few ducks out on the water in that time that I found it hard to imagine the nests would ever be used. But Anna said we didn't know which ones the ducks would choose, so we should just make them all as well as we could, even if only a few of them got used. She had the final say about each nest, whether it was built right or not. Sometimes she would remake one that Ingrid or I had just finished. She'd seen a flaw with it that we hadn't, often something so small that even after she'd remade it we were none the wiser.

'I would not want to sit there,' she said, about one nest I'd made.

It was in a well-lit spot near the pop-hole through which the ducks came and went. I learned that ducks that nested in such places were most likely to be killed or disturbed. Mink or otter might crawl halfway in and snatch a bird or an egg. Years of wisdom informed Anna's work; endless mishaps and setbacks told her what was likely to go wrong and where. Anna moved my nest further in from the little entrance hole and remade it.

I asked Anna how the ducks had ever survived in the wild, if they were so vulnerable here. Out there, Anna said, pointing to the north, the mother would find somewhere on the foreshore, just above the tides, where she could build a nest from dried seaweed. When the last eggs of the brood were laid, she sat on them for twenty-six – sometimes twenty-seven – days until they hatched. While she sat, she was vulnerable, relying on little more than her brown mottled plumage to keep her hidden in the shadows of the rocks. A bird scientist told Anna that on Svalbard, in the wild north, up to 80 per cent of wild eider-duck eggs were taken by predators. That figure might have been lower in the past. The ducks perhaps did better in healthy oceans, with vast numbers of other seabirds creating a commotion at nesting places that deterred predators. In the past, when there were more people, and guns and traps, there had been fewer predators, like otters and eagles. There were certainly no North American mink. It was hard to understand the ocean, its vast chains of causes and effects, its cycles of boom and bust. Even the scientists were vague. But for Anna it was simple: without our help these ducks would be in big trouble.

~

Just a week earlier, a fear had hung over us that we might not be ready for the ducks. I had been daunted by the sheer number of nests needed, and worried that we were going to fail in our task. But by making twenty to thirty nests a day – a target that Ingrid had been steadily keeping us to – we were now on schedule. Many of the key nesting places were ready. And because there was still no sign of the ducks, and their coming-in took several days, Anna now knew that we would get it all done.

Ingrid hadn't said so to me, but she had arranged to go to her daughter's place on the mainland for a few days. Anna insisted she go back on the boat with Henrik when he came as planned, and Ingrid was relieved. I understood that she was tired and had been worried that this short trip home would not be possible.

The two women hugged on the wharf, and, as Ingrid left, she gave Anna a look that said, 'Stay safe, and don't do anything foolish.' Then she looked to me as if to say, 'Take care of my friend,' and I smiled as reassuringly as I could.

~

The next morning, fog blew in from the sea, muffling the noise of the ocean waves, and the island felt small and quiet. I followed Anna as she walked down the meadow, through the tussocks silvered with tiny droplets of mist. The acidic yellow flowers of the water marigold now brightened the hollows and damp places. She was on her way to Ship Island, the little mound of rock that rose from the sea down in front of the house. We looked to this place all the time, from the sofa and the kitchen window. These were the most watched nests – their every drama would be visible to us. It was also where I had first seen Anna, all those years earlier.

Anna climbed down the jagged foreshore, with its grey volcanic rocks full of swirls and ulcers. Tiny plants sheltered in the cracks. She stepped carefully across low places full of slimy seaweed and up the rocks again. She knew that a bad fall would be the end of her island days; old bones break easily, like biscuits. But she was careful, and wanted to make these final nests.

~

Ship Island had no large huts or barns. There were three or four wooden packing-boxes and several ancient, stone-walled structures that would hold the nests. Ingrid and I had carried the boxes and wooden nest-fronts there a few days earlier.

The winter storms had battered all the stone nests, tumbling them into themselves. A stranger might have wondered what these little cairns were. Anna chose one and lifted the tumbled stones out of the centre, tossing them to the side, where they landed with a crack. She scraped out the damp, black soil in the middle, and then began to rebuild the nest. From the stones she had cleared out, she now chose the largest ones and used them to build a crude, drystone-walled C.

When she was short of a stone or two, she went to the foreshore or a rockpool edge to find what she needed. The rockpools were full of broken shells of sea urchins. The biggest stones she used were the size of a bread loaf, others were no bigger than a coffee mug. She made the wall solid, filling cracks to keep the daylight out. The structure was soon almost up to her knees. She checked the top stones wouldn't fall, or panic a duck by wobbling in the wind. She laid each rock down thoughtfully, like we would when building a drystone wall at home.

I started on another cairn a few steps away, and Anna watched me as she worked. She said, 'You have done this before,' and I said I hadn't, but had built many drystone walls with my father and grandfather, and these were the same skills. When I was done, she showed me how to secure the top layer of rocks, and then nodded for me to start on the next mound a few metres away.

When we had both built another external wall, she showed me the next stage: making the roof. She set two or three lengths of driftwood across the wall tops – these would be the beams.

Anna was fully in her element now, absorbed in the work. A thousand years ago, Viking women would have built nests just like these, using only what could be salvaged from the foreshore. She took a square of plywood and set it down as the floor. She built on this a mat of dried seaweed, then laid a green circle of rope to hold the nest in place. She filled that with small loose bits of seaweed that she pressed in with her fingers. Then she tucked the wooden front in place under the roof timbers and laid on a final stone or two to hold roof and front together. Each wooden front had a nest name scribbled on the back with marker pen. The front was a fat-legged H with the top arch filled in, and the bottom left open. She told me the entrance had to be 11 centimetres high, or it was 'no good'.

Lastly, a large armful of seaweed was laid on top of it all, like the camouflage on a soldier's helmet. She stood back with her hands on her hips and smiled. Then she leaned a stone against the front to hold it firm. She told me that the blasted ravens had learnt to pull the nest out and feed on the eggs or the ducklings.

We worked for a couple of hours. Side by side. I was proud of my work. The walls were good. Anna inspected each one, making finishing tweaks.

Two geese watched us from the water. They seemed to rest here round the nest mounds during the day. The rocks we knelt on were covered in swirls of their shit, which looked like it had been squeezed out of a tube of toothpaste.

We headed back to the house. An hour or two later the tide flowed in, and Ship Island, now speckled with ancient-looking stone and seaweed mounds, was separated from us by fifty feet of glassy ocean. I felt a quiet elation. The distance between Anna and I had shrunk to nothing.

~

We sat in the kitchen, watching the sea in silence. Soon, only the centre of Ship Island remained above the tide. Anna told me that she'd persuaded the ducks to come back to her family's island, Måsøy, by building nests like the ones we'd made that day: old stone, driftwood, and seaweed. I was still confused about that – about why we were on Fjærøy, not Måsøy — and what could have happened to tear her from that place that was clearly so sacred to her, just as our farm was to us. But I didn't ask anything more.

Later that afternoon we were moving timber in the barn. I said it was good that she was able to work again, and she smiled in agreement. She found some bits of tin that she said would be great for the roofs of wooden nest boxes and told me to set them to one side. A week ago, she had barely been able to lift herself from the sofa, and now she was tossing wood about and hardly needed me. I said she was stronger than she looked. She said she had always surprised people, quite literally since the day she was born.

Her mother had been bewildered when the midwife had handed her a baby girl, as though she'd been given the wrong bag of groceries in the shop. There must be a mistake, she said, because she had knitted a pile of blue baby clothes. She was sure she was having a boy. Then the midwife said there was another baby coming. He came with a roar. Tore. The chubby boy she had expected.

The doctor had told Ulka that she would be having twins, but she'd chosen not to believe him — and hadn't told her husband. They had just enough room at home for one new baby and she was determined it would be a boy.

Anna and Tore had shared the blue baby clothes, even though they were much too big for Anna. Anna's father said she was the 'bonus girl' that no one had expected.

He stuck up for her. If Tore got too big for his boots, he always reminded him that Anna was the eldest.

Her mother didn't have enough milk for two babies, so they hired a seventeen-year-old girl from the village to be Anna's wet nurse. She was called Emma and was married to their friend, 'Little' Kasper. Emma loved Anna so much she wanted to keep her with her own baby. Anna thought perhaps her mother might have agreed, but Anna's father said no.

~

I put two logs on the fire, and Anna talked of her children. She spoke to her daughters on the phone, but said it was not the same as being together. She wished they could come here and be duck women, and then reminded herself they had their own lives. She was proud of them. Amalie was kind and thoughtful, and a worrier, like her father. Mari was perhaps more like her mum, wilful, with her emotions near the surface. They came whenever they got time off and sometimes brought their boyfriends. Anna said Oslo swallowed up young people and wouldn't let them go. It seemed to me that, like young people everywhere, they perhaps didn't know how to come home, or what they'd do if they did.

Anna asked me how I'd ended up back at our family farm after leaving it to go to university. I explained that in my heart I'd never really left, never really fitted in anywhere else. I said perhaps I was foolish, unable to move on from such an old-fashioned way of living. But Anna wasn't having it. There was nothing old-fashioned about that, she said. Her daughters would come back someday. They loved the islands, too.

~

The work happened in waves, each stage rippling out across the sea estate. We'd started making nests on the main island, near the house, then moved on to the skerries and islets we could walk to at low tide, and finished with the places that required the little boat. Now we were going out to the furthest place, South Island, and its cluster of surrounding islets, for the last of the nest-building.

As we went down the path to the boat, two little birds, rock pippets, rose from grass. I noticed that Fjærøy was different now from when we had first come. It got greener with each passing day, no longer desolate, and I felt more at home. In the abandoned garden behind the house, the rhubarb was emerging from the debris of last summer, like tiny green lumps of coral with spearheads that were beginning to show pink.

Anna seemed nervous. The sea was powerful. The tidal currents, even between the little islands and skerries, were wicked. The distances were tiny, but the wind could whip through the channels and sweep a boat out to the deep sea or towards the rocks. I remembered that in Anna's island stories everyone drowned.

Ingrid pretended to Stig that she never used the little rowing boat, Anna said. She made out that she didn't know how to. Anna seemed to be implying that Ingrid slotted into what other people expected of her too much. Or perhaps she was telling me that Ingrid was tougher than people gave her credit for. I couldn't tell.

That morning it seemed calm enough to me. The wind had dropped, and the sea was still. The yellow rowing boat was tied on a running line where it could bob gently up and down on the tides, safe in the inlet. Anna pulled the rope and brought the boat in close, until it scraped the rocks. She stepped aboard in her life jacket and baled out scoops of water. She waited for me to climb in, a little awkwardly, and then pushed away. The oars dipped into the water and we glided to the first islet, which she called South Rock.

We were soon out of the boat and clambering up the triangle of granite. It was littered on the far side with timbers. There was an oystercatcher's nest in a little patch of gravel between some boulders. The eggs were warm. Anna rebuilt a stone duck hut. She pointed to half a dozen eider ducks on the water, a hundred feet away in an inlet, and a couple of other pairs hanging about on distant skerries. I stared at them in wonder. These birds we had worked so hard to welcome, but then they were gone again. The group nearest us drifted away. Anna led us back down the foreshore quietly. We were finishing the nests just in time.

Three or four strokes got us over to South Island. It

was the biggest of the islands in the *vær*. It was the shape of an almond and surrounded by a large foreshore of brown and grey rocks. The headlands were covered in dead grass, yellow and tangled with the juniper.

Anna went ahead, across a wide plateau of rock, a tiny stick-woman in a vast seascape. There were broken goose eggs by the path and a little bay full of seaweed and debris. She led us to some nest huts on a headland a hundred metres away. On the way, she showed me a pile of feathers: the remains of a goose killed by a sea eagle. She said an ancient tug-of-war took place here each day between those that would bring their young into the world, and those that killed them to live. The whole sea estate was like a watery Serengeti.

We got to the furthest nest boxes, opened them up, and began building. This island could have housed many more nests, Anna said, and perhaps once had done, but there was only so much we could do with the time we had. We made perhaps twenty nests in total there, in various places, before Anna said we were done.

The sun was shining. We sat on the headland and rested. I asked if the ducks would come quickly now, and she shrugged. Things happened when they happened in Anna's world, and only fools asked too many questions.

Anna wandered down to the sea. She knelt in front of some of the stone nest houses and peered in.

Anna's life here was, I was coming to see, devoted to paying attention to – or, more than that, being completely committed to – the beauty of the world before her. She seemed to have done it by cultivating an extraordinary form of independence from other people, their values, and their noise. She used every ounce of her wilfulness to shut out the world and concentrate on these simple things.

More and more, she reminded me of my grandfather. He spent many hours walking his farm and learning about the wild things upon it, like it was the most important work a human could do. Growing up, I'd wanted to be like him. And I was, for three or four years, after I left school. I'd go for walks over the fields; on sunny nights I'd sit with my back against a rock or climb into the lower branches of a tree and watch the world happening around me. I'd spend hours just watching deer or foxes or badgers, or swifts tumbling and screaming through the sky. I'd lie on my back in the grass and watch the swallows hawking after flies round my dad's cows, or the brown hares playing in the meadows. But somewhere in the years since, I'd stopped being that person. Life was too busy to stand and stare. I became responsible for boring, necessary things. At one point I had three jobs and worked most nights and weekends. D. H. Lawrence once wrote that the industrial age had created a new kind of human, a machine-like man with iron in his soul. I had become one of them. The past few years had been swallowed up by striving. I remembered a friend back home trying to tell me, gently, that I had become almost manic. But the longer I spent with Anna, the more that way of being felt like a sickness I needed to recover from. A new calmness began to settle over me. It was a feeling I had not known since I was a child following my grandfather round his fields.

Anna reminded me that the first rule of living is to live. To see, hear, smell, touch, and taste the world. The more I tuned in, the closer Anna and I were growing as friends. I was beginning a journey back to the person I had once been – and needed to be again.

4.

Varntid

After three or four days, Ingrid returned on Henrik's boat. She looked fresh and clean, and, when she hugged me, I realized that I wasn't. There was no bath or shower on the island, and no washing machine, so as the weeks passed, we got a little grubby. On rare sunny days we'd each wash some of our clothes by hand in a bucket. Ingrid had seen our stone nests on Ship Island from the boat and was impressed. It felt good to get her back, our strange island family complete again.

That night the fire was roaring in the living room. Anna held a glass to the cardboard wine box on the table and pressed the little button until it was full of red. Ingrid copied her. Anna opened the chocolate mints Ingrid had brought back, and they picked one each, then passed them to me. Ingrid said Anna looked much better. She said she had seen many more eiders beginning to gather far out on the sea.

~

The next few days were spent doing odd jobs, because we were almost ready for the coming of the ducks. There was a feeling of expectation in the air. Each morning we went out and peered at the ocean in hope.

The women seemed to trust me now – to trust that I knew the rules of the place, and had become quiet and observant enough to do no harm. I felt at home now and part of everything. I had even slowed my walk to be like Anna's. To be most useful, I went to places she couldn't get to, like Crow Island, and I'd sit and watch what the seabirds were doing, or what boats were out there, and later report back to her. I saw more barnacle geese pass overhead. I knew they'd come back from the Solway Estuary near to my home and were on their way north. Anna called them Svalbard geese – we found them in her bird guide. Sometimes, I would tell her about a crow or a distant boat, and she would smile at me, like she'd made the right decision trusting me to be there.

~

The peace didn't last long. In those days before the ducks came, the island was busy with people coming and going.

Henrik arrived late one morning. Through the kitchen window, I watched his boat creating a contrail of white foam as it cut across the dark blue of the bay. He had brought groceries. He came up the path for a coffee, and we sat on the decking – but no one seemed to be in the mood for talking. Henrik went back to his boat, because he said he had a few jobs to do on it before he left. Then we heard another boat chug in through the channel. Anna sighed wearily.

'Another man. Perfect.'

Ingrid said it was Lars. His boat was towing another boat that sat low in the water, because it was loaded with timber.

Anna said, 'We'll never bloody get rid of him.'

We heard barking. The two men's dogs were fighting on the jetty. Henrik grabbed his little white dog and swung a boot at Lars's German shepherd, and was soon heading home.

Lars appeared at the back door. A grey-haired man with a kind face, wearing many layers of shirts and jumpers. He said he had come to mend one of the barns for Terje. Anna told him sharply that he would upset the coming ducks with his dog making such a racket. It was no time for his clattering and hammering. He didn't seem to care. He followed her inside and settled into an armchair. Anna threw up her hands as she went into the kitchen.

Anna had told me that in her early years of working with the ducks she had spent long periods on her own. It seemed to me that was what she truly loved. Just her and the ducks, out on the rocks far from other people. Getting old seemed to have softened that independence. I felt a little sorry for her: she seemed plagued with people, and had to suffer them because it wasn't her island.

After a coffee, Lars sailed his boat full of timber round the headland, to the sea barn in a tiny inlet between the rocks. It was a bright orange boat, that he used to help farmers take their sheep out to the islands. At high tide he sailed it as far up the beach as he could, then, as the tide receded, he propped it there with timbers to stop it from tipping over, leaving it high and dry up in the inlet. When the tide was fully out it looked like Noah's Ark, before the deluge. Anna came for a look.

'Do you think you have propped it up enough, Lars?'

He didn't answer. We left him unloading timber, taking it across the rocks and up into the loft of the barn. The whole noisy exercise drove Anna mad. The handful of ducks now gathering off the headlands showed their displeasure by paddling away. She was incredulous that he would use this much timber. Terje only needed a new barn front, not for Lars to open a lumber yard. She said Lars was impossible.

Once, she told me, he'd arrived with a broken gear-box that had left his boat stuck in reverse, and Ingrid had had to pull him in with a rope. Another time he came at low tide and tied the ropes too tight, and, when the water rose, the increasingly taut rope slowly tipped the boat over, so seawater poured in. He'd been working across the island, oblivious. But Anna had heard a mechanical whining noise while working in one of the huts, and realized that the boat's electric pump had started to bail out water. She went down to the jetty and saw the boat filling, soaking his food and half-flooding the cabin that was his bedroom.

~

It took Lars the best part of three days to get his timber unloaded. We spent those days finishing the last few nests with seaweed that was so brittle it crumbled into shards, which pricked and scratched our swollen hands. The ducks hung about on the water and distant skerries, biding their time.

I learned that Anna had known Lars for many years. He'd been an engineer on the mainland until he retired, when he'd taken up carpentry work for Terje, and had slowly earned his trust. He was allowed to hunt around the islands and became a steward, of sorts, of the property. Anna told me that the first time she came to Fjærøyvær, Lars happened to be there, working on the barns. She'd come with the previous duck woman, Emma, for a hand-over, learning about the nests, and where everything was kept. Lars seemed to think he was in charge. He had asked her what time she would make breakfast, and she'd laughed at him.

'I think he thought I was to be his housemaid.'

Now, when he came, he stayed on his boat at night, but had his meals in the house, and enjoyed telling stories by the stove, about the war, shipwrecks, and hunting.

~

Anna always kept one eye on the sea. She'd fix like a hawk on boats coming to the island from miles away, and watch nervously as they got closer. She'd often draw our attention to a dot on the waves, far out, and would say whose boat she thought it was, and whether it was coming to our island or another.

Whenever someone docked and stepped ashore Anna would recoil slightly, like the island was an extension of her body and someone had touched it, uninvited. I thought it odd the first time I saw it, but soon I reacted in the same way.

All visitors irritated Anna, but unannounced visitors were the worst of all. When other people were with us, Anna seemed to find it a struggle, being polite and going through the motions. She would usually be the quietest person in the room. I would often see other people try and take liberties. But slowly I recognized that her silence was a defence against their blustering. She was always firm. Anna seemed to sense that I'd noticed this, and now and again she'd catch my eye and smile, as if grateful for a witness.

~

On his fourth day Lars worked on the barn. He rebuilt the front wall with treated pine planks that neatly over-lapped, and crafted a new window-surround. The ledge would guide rain down and away from the window frame.

After lunch, he was suddenly, and suspiciously, very focused. He even cut short his coffee break. Anna said, 'He's definitely up to something.'

'If he always worked this hard he would make an

excellent husband,' Ingrid said, winking at Anna, who laughed and said if she had to live with him she'd probably kill him, and she pulled her finger across her throat for comic effect.

The days were lengthening, and the sun shone right into the evening. Anna pointed out the window: some ducks were gathering at a distance. We took turns watching them with the binoculars, passing them to each other to see. I could see dark silhouettes on distant skerries and rafts of seaweed. Some formed groups of half a dozen or so, drifting in and out on the wide tidal channels. Our binoculars were full of them, duck-like dots everywhere. And then the wind changed, and they drifted out of sight. Anna went for a short walk, and came back excited about how many she had seen beyond the headland.

~

The women were washing up in the kitchen when Lars reappeared and whispered to me. Would I like to go *out*? The way he said 'out' made me think he meant on his boat. Anna and Ingrid seemed relaxed, and not to be going back out to work, so I nodded. He told them we were going out, and was gone before they could say any more. 'Wonderful World' by Louis Armstrong was on the radio. As I put on my boots, Anna came to the porch. She said she knew what he was up to. He must have been wanting to get his work done in time to allow himself a trip out to the wilder islets a mile or two away, before he had to go home. He could do no harm to her ducks out there. She told me to have fun, but to make sure he didn't drown me.

~

Lars kept his gaze on a cluster of distant islands on the horizon. The outboard motor purred as we went further and further out, to rocks where no one lived or worked. The setting sun cast the islands and the water in a soft glow. After twenty minutes or so, we reached an island. He nudged the boat in among the rocks, until it bellied on the gravel. Our boots crunched up the deep drifts of seaweed, thrown up by the highest tides. The seaweed was rotting and smelled of sulphur. We walked through the rubbish vomited up by the choking sea. There were blue plastic ropes, tennis balls, green and white torn fishing nets, cyclists' reusable water bottles, and endless Coke, Fanta, and Pepsi bottles.

A few strides up from the foreshore, the upper shore-line was covered in roseroot, with its little golden heads. Soon we were among the dwarf juniper bushes, twenty or so feet above sea level, their branches clawing like fingers across the rock faces. Lars found a grassy ledge covered with giant white and brown feathers where eagles had torn up their kills. But there was no nest.

We went back to the boat and Lars worked his way from island to island, until we had been ashore several times. He reminded me of an otter, equally at home on the waves or the rocks.

He said he was looking for sea eagle nests. But I could tell he also wanted to show me the place he knew and loved. He told me he came out several times a year, in all seasons. He went to Fjærøy when the house was empty, and Anna was at home on Vega working on the eiderdown.

Lars sailed us further out across the ocean, into the light. It was not hard to see why he came. There was a beauty here that filled the eyes and the heart. Seals poked their heads up in the distance, and immediately dropped them again. He told me he had been coming to these islands his whole life, hunting for seal, mink, and otters, or fishing with his friends. He said you had to have your wits about you out here, in bad weather. He said you had to eat seal fresh, because the flesh didn't keep. At times, in winter, he had been so frozen he'd warmed his hands in the blubber of a seal. He knew how to sneak up on geese using the wind. He knew how to feed his family from the sea.

I showed him a photo of my wife and told him she was worried about me out here. She'd messaged me earlier that day. He said his wife had also worried about him being out on the sea alone. She had said he wasn't a young man any more. As he spoke about her, his eyes sparkled. She'd been the junior swimming champion of Norway. He couldn't believe she'd fallen in love with him. She had come to Vega from Bergen to marry him, and they shared a good life on the farm. She taught people to swim, including Anna, who, embarrassed that she couldn't, had asked to learn in the municipal swimming pool when no one was watching. But now his wife was gone, Lars said. So he wasn't scared of getting old, or having an accident out at sea, if it meant he got to see her again.

It was good to go out with Lars. I couldn't help but like him. He was full of playfulness, and being with him was one long adventure. He reminded me of my childhood when we had roamed for miles to catch fish in little streams, and the whole world was no bigger than where we could get with our bicycles.

On the last island he found a sea eagle's nest from last year – a two-metre-wide pile of rotten sticks and bare earth – but it seemed to have been abandoned. I took a giant quill for Anna's jar in the house.

We headed back in the half-light. Cormorants passed by, fast and low, on the straightest of lines. Lars said he should really have finished the barn this evening, but what was the hurry, the women were going to fry fish tomorrow.

There was now no real darkness, but the sky was greying. When we were almost back to Fjærøy we saw a heron – it was being watched by two gulls. It stabbed down with its beak into a rock pool, then threw back its head with something worm-like dangling from the side of its beak. The gulls hopped closer in anticipation, but the heron swallowed its catch whole.

The light out at sea now had a strange quality, changing the colours of things at twilight. The water never looked the same twice, like someone was constantly changing the filters on a photograph.

At the quayside I said goodnight to Lars, who sloped down to his boat, and I went back to the house where the two women were still talking. Anna wanted a full report. Ingrid seemed relieved that I was back in one piece.

~

The next morning at breakfast Anna scolded Lars, said he must get his work on the barn finished. He looked irritated but headed out, and we soon heard banging and sawing. Anna said, 'I think he would like to be here all the time.'

Then she raised an eyebrow and shook her head to make clear that wasn't going to happen. They washed up, and soon seemed to forget about him. I went down to the barn to see if he needed a hand, but he was focused on his work and would barely chat. All day Anna watched the ducks from her perch on the sofa. Some were now in pairs out on the bay. Lars came in occasionally for coffee, but didn't stay long. He was making her anxious and short-tempered.

Late that afternoon, he came to the house holding a piece of cloth to his face. His nose was bust and trickling dark, clotting blood. He'd been using a hammer and it had bounced up and hit him on the nose, he explained. Ingrid told him to sit. His cheeks were smeared with strawberry-coloured blood now. She stopped the bleeding with a clean cloth, then put a bandage round his head. He looked to be rather enjoying the fuss.

Anna was now beyond exasperated. She busied herself boiling potatoes, and dipping fish in flour and frying it in butter. Lars said it smelled delicious. We sat around the little table. He pricked a potato from the boiling pan, peeled off its purple earthy skin, and set it on a saucer. Anna did the same. Lars asked if they had any beer. Anna went to the door and threw her hands up in the air behind him, mouthing silent obscenities. She brought back some pale blue cans of lager. Lars's green beer glass cast a shadow on the white table mat. After we had eaten, he went back through to the comfy seats, and we all sat and chatted. They told me how hard it had been to get liquor in Norway in their youth.

Lars said that, years ago, two immigrants who'd worked as labourers on the sea defences to the south had heard that a passing ship had liquor for sale. They rowed out and bought some, and then got roaring drunk. They were so inebriated they fell asleep and lost their oars. They'd drifted for two or three days up the coast on the current. Eventually they washed ashore on a skerry near to Vega. They had quenched their thirst from rainwater pools on the rocks and eaten seabird eggs. They had terrible sunburn. A fisherman had seen them waving like lunatics. He'd shouted to them that he couldn't get ashore there because it was too rocky, but they'd been hysterical. When he got closer, they swam out and almost drowned him clambering into his boat. He took them back to Vega.

The setting sun flooded the room with light. The Jaffa Cakes in the glass bowl on the table had a melted sheen on one side where the sun had caught them. Later, we drank Jägermeister by candlelight and Lars told stories about the war. As a boy, he knew many of the local men who had been in the resistance. They'd had illegal radios on the islands, caches of weapons and explosives, and had smuggled people in and out of the country. Some of the fishermen had spent the war on Orkney, or had gone further south to make plans with their king and his people in his hotel in London. Lars said that after the war the local men kept their networks, and their wartime heroism, quiet in case the Russians invaded and they were needed again.

Anna told Lars about the otter smell in one of the huts. He said he almost trod on an otter there a few years ago. It had been hiding from his hunting dog. It hissed at him, then bolted for the waves and was gone.

He said the otter would have to be shot. Ingrid said the authorities wouldn't allow that. 'Huh,' Lars grunted. 'The coast of Norway goes on forever. There are no end of otters. They can have the rest of it. And, besides, the conservation people aren't here. What they don't know won't hurt them.'

Anna asked if Lars would finish the barn soon. He

didn't seem to hear. Her hand tightened into a fist on the armrest of her sofa. He looked as though he was miles away. Then he jerked back into focus, sensing he was pushing it, said goodnight, and went back to his boat.

~

At breakfast Anna told Lars that the growing number of ducks on the water were being disturbed by his banging and he really must go. Now. She didn't think he was listening, but after a brief flurry of activity loading and putting his tools away, and getting the sheep boat out again, he left. There was no real goodbye; Lars was there one minute and gone the next. Anna said to Ingrid, 'I guess we're painting the new front on the barn then,' and they both laughed.

~

Men, Anna said as Lars left, could not be quiet. We must now stay inside and let the ducks do their coming ashore. Anna watched their every move from the window. They edged closer to the land, drifting in and out on the tide. They were starting to find mates and decide which islands looked trustworthy. We had completed the nest-making, and now it was time to be quiet so they could come.

This period of silence was enshrined in the old coastal laws. It was called the *varntid* (pronounced 'varn-tee').

Ships had to lower their canvas sails to prevent them flapping and scaring away the birds. Fisherman were told not to come close to the islands with their motor-boats. The ducks came to land in painfully shy stages – it could take a duck a week to build up the courage simply to set a webbed foot on the shore. And they wouldn't all do it together; a few would come each day, so that, from the first bird until the last, the landing would be stag-gered over three or four weeks – from mid-May to mid-June. They were easily frightened away from the nesting places, and even from their eggs.

On arrival, they would be so shy, and their trust in the island so tenuous, that we would spend much of our time hiding away from them in the house. *Varntid* lasted until the eiders hatched their ducklings and went back to the sea. It was our job to be quiet, and police the silence.

Anna got me doing jobs around the house, mending curtain rails or shelves. She'd sit on the sofa as I worked and give me instructions. I asked her if this whole duck thing was legit, or just a hoax to get Englishmen to do her DIY. I knew she wouldn't mind this teasing, though once she might have. She had told me she spent much of her early life proving she was as tough as the boys and men around her.

Her brother had grown up strong and healthy, but she had fallen behind like a runt. They called her 'the doll' at school because she was so pale. Her mother made her wear a second pair of tights to make her legs look thicker. Her family became scared and took her to the doctor, who diagnosed her with anaemia. He said they must get more iron into Anna, to thicken her blood. There were pills, he said, but they were too strong for someone so delicate, and would destroy the girl's teeth. Her parents decided to care for her without the medicine. They kept her away from things that would exhaust her, stopped her carrying heavy buckets or timber to her father whilst he built the house. Her mother fed her as much lamb and beef as they could afford. In time, Anna built up her strength and was able to follow behind the other island children as they roamed the woods and headlands on Vega. She became irritated at everyone fussing around her.

One day her brother was sent to cut the meadow with a sickle. Her father, busy in the barn, said she was still too weak to help in the field and should go and help her mother in the kitchen. Anna was furious. She felt she could do anything her brother could do. So she stole the old scythe from the byre and went to mow beside him. They began to race, and, though Tore could swing the blade faster, she soon got a rhythm and could match him with the bigger blade. When their father came to the field, they were both sweating and covered in grass seeds, worn out, but neither yielding an inch. Anna's brother looked shaken, relieved to stop and lay down his sickle. But she was full of adrenaline, feeling like she could do another field on her own. Her whole life after that, she had hated being told she couldn't do things. Me too, I said, I hate that. 'Well, you will have to do as I tell you, and stop talking when the ducks come up to the nests,' she said. She needn't have worried. I was here to do as I was told and we both knew who was in charge.

~

Waiting for the ducks to come to the island was like the scene in the film *The Longest Day* where German soldiers wait in Normandy for the D-Day invasion. The soldiers in the pillboxes facing out to sea had the most boring job in the war, spending endless days staring out for a thing that might be spectacular when it happened, but which never seemed to come. Except we weren't waiting for battleships, but ducks.

We spent hours gazing out to the wild, grey sea.

The tides came and went.

The clouds raced over.

The water flowed up the channels, and then back out. Gulls rose and fell on the gusts. The ducks seemed unsure whether to come ashore or not. I worked my way through the pile of books I'd brought with me to the island. The wind howled at the windows. The world shrank to such elemental things. The jumper Anna was knitting slowly grew beneath her needles. Ingrid was knitting some socks with two balls of wool, one creamy white and the other grey. Anna had two balls of wool, one pink and one white, nestled by her thigh.

It took a certain kind of person to stay on a duck island in the quiet times, Anna told me. Silence bothered people. They were so used to noise and babbling on that they couldn't wait to fill it.

Ingrid told me she had once spent a week alone on the island while Anna went home to do her washing and shop for supplies. It had rained all week, and the wind had blown. Absolutely nothing had happened. No ducks. Nothing. When Anna got back, she met Ingrid coming down the path in the opposite direction, bags in hand. The solitude had driven her half mad. She went home on the boat for a hot bath and a few days on Vega.

Anna was different. She had the right nature for being a duck woman. She was inherently quiet and modest, but also extremely determined. She began to tell me, in instalments, about her early years as a duck woman on Måsøy. She had spent whole seasons in silence waiting, alone, for ducks that never came. She had devoted years of unpaid work to persuading a few ducks to trust her and come home, sustained only by an unshakeable belief that it could be done, and that it mattered.

One afternoon, as we watched the first ducks bickering on the foreshore and others splashing in the bay, Anna told me it was magical when the birds trusted an island. When she had started – on Måsøy – it hadn't been like this. The ducks had all but abandoned the place in her father's last years.

When Anna went for her very first season, nearly thirty years earlier, she'd hoped that her presence on the island – along with the new nests she would build – would be enough to entice them back. There is science behind this: humans create a 'shadow of fear' that keeps predators away, and ducks have worked out that being in this shadow is a good idea. But Anna couldn't exactly send the wild ducks a letter telling them it was safe to return.

That first year she had help from Henning, and Mari had stayed out there with her. They rebuilt the nests on the main island, and in all the other places her father had told her about. She watched the ducks pairing up on the water and spent days willing them up the channel. She'd talk to them quietly from the other side of the glass: 'Come and try my perfect new nests that I built for you.' But no ducks came ashore. They no longer trusted the island.

After a month, her leave from work ran out and she went home with almost nothing to show for her efforts. When she got the chance to go back out one weekend, she found that a couple of ducks had been killed in the nests she'd made on the main island. She felt deeply guilty. She had made them inviting homes and then failed to stick around to protect them. She realized that she either had to give up the whole dream or stay out there for the entire nesting season. But it was more than just being there. Anna knew she had to do something more to bring the birds back.

Her father and brother said maybe the eiders would never come again. But giving up wasn't Anna's style.

She needed a new plan.

She spoke to the handful of older people who had kept the work going on their own ancestral islands. Some were convinced the tradition was doomed. They saw themselves as the last of their kind. Some, particularly the old men, were almost proud to be taking their knowledge to the grave with them. Anna thought that was stupid: knowledge was for passing on, not burying; for the living, not the dead. Others, though, shared what they knew.

Anna made it her work to study not just the ducks but their environment, learning about the tides, winds, changing clouds, the light, the behaviour of the different seabirds. She learned to watch carefully. One day, she saw a large and idle white gull, out in the calmer water of the bay, begin to screech and flap. Something yanked it beneath the surface. It came back up, terrified, flailing for the sky. A juvenile killer whale had the gull by its foot, and was playing with it, allowing it to come up for air, then taking it back under. The game went on until the screaming gull drowned and the whale moved with its pod around the ragged shore. Another time, she saw what she thought was a ship's sail flash far out at sea, before realizing it was the spray from a giant breaching whale. She recorded all this in her diary. Often she noted down sightings of 'auntie' ducks – unpaired females that formed their own gangs – passing the sea barn on the open water, or by the shore or the pond. Anna connected herself to it all. She began to think like a duck, and, after a while, the penny dropped. If the ducks wouldn't come to her, she would have to go to them.

There were a small number of wild nests on the place they called Flat Skerry. It was a short rowing-boat journey from the main island of Måsøy, just a plateau of rock a little above sea level. The rock was home to a seagull colony, which meant that when a mink, otter, skua, or crow came ashore, all hell broke loose. Hundreds of gulls and terns screamed and dive-bombed the predator back to the sky or sea. Here, the ducks still felt safe enough to nest.

Anna's people had harvested down from these wild nests, but never attempted to build nests there. She decided she would try to get the ducks used to her, and to stone nests, by building around their eggs. Their numbers would grow, and they'd come to trust humans again. Over time, half-tame to her presence, they'd drift back to the main island.

It was a simple plan. But it was also little more than a fantasy. No one she knew had done this before – at least not in living memory.

Still, Anna was convinced she could revive the eiderdown station. She felt that she owed it to the ducks. And she believed she could recreate the glory of what had once been. She would turn back the clock, however hard it was, however long it took.

I asked her, 'What did everyone think about your plan?'

'They thought I was crazy.'

'Was that why you left Måsøy, because no ducks came?'

'No,' she replied. 'The plan worked.'

~

The inlets around Fjærøy began to fill with ducks: six, eight, fifteen . . . until they were bobbing about everywhere, or resting on the rafts of seaweed and the half-submerged shelves of rock. Brown female ducks preened themselves beside the white males, often in pairs, feathers ruffling in the shallow water. Then the scattered pairs on the water became little groups of half a dozen. Soon, the bay was crowded with ducks. Anna stood by the window, stretching to see more of the bay and the channel. The colour was back in her cheeks. Our island shantytown of empty nests was waiting for feathered tenants. But the ducks were shy and cautious, and days passed without them coming in. Once a day, the three of us checked the nests – that was the drill. Anna would judge the right time for this. Ingrid and I would follow her out, and we'd make our way to the huts, watching we didn't disturb the ducks, either on the water or on their way up to a nest. Days passed. We found nothing nesting.

We all believed the birds would come ashore, but they had made no promises. Everything about the ducks' coming was tentative. They'd take two strokes closer to land, then five strokes back to the sea when they saw anything to make them nervous. The women told me that the number of ducks coming to Fjærøyvær was falling. The old records said there had been 1,300 eiders in the spring of 1900. That had dropped to 400 birds a century later, when a woman called Sigrid had cared for them. The annual total of nests was now written on a beam in the barn in marker pen – I could see it had fallen below 200 nests a few years ago, and now Anna was struggling to get much over 120. This was a pretty desperate collapse.

I asked Anna if she ever worried about the sea. She sighed. For years, she said, Henning had been telling her that the sea was dying. He'd show anyone who'd listen scientific graphs of the sand-eel population crashing in the 1970s. He'd moan about the little fish hoovered up by industrial fishing boats in the Atlantic and fish stocks collapsing. He said the seabirds were starving. No one really listened. Anna had been impatient with such gloominess – it was just like men to believe their every thought mattered. She was focused on doing. But recently, she told me, she'd gone to a meeting on Vega with the bird scientists. They'd said the sea was changing, doing strange things. They seemed scared, but also unsure what it meant. They'd asked her what she thought was happening, which she found troubling. Didn't *they* know?

To Anna, the situation was simple. There were many more ducks nesting and rearing chicks where they were cared for and protected than in places where they had to fend for themselves. Our responsibility was clear: we had to make the nests and stand guard over them. After that we could only wait and see what would happen.

Anna gave me a look. 'They will come, you will see,' she said. She seemed to distrust and be irritated by despair, like it was a waste of energy. However badly broken the sea might be, you just had to put one foot in front of the other, make each nest, one by one.

~

In the second year she went to Måsøy, Anna put her plan into practice. She found a wild nest with five eggs hidden in the seaweed on Flat Skerry. She built a stone house around the nest. She was nervous about whether the duck would suffer this new home or abandon it. But when she went back to check, the mother bird was sitting calmly and didn't even flinch when she peered in. This was a 'workable' duck. She soon found another duck that had laid eggs, and made a house for her, too, which she also accepted. Soon these ducks would let Anna reach under them on their nests to check their eggs. Anna learned how to move around them so gradually that they accepted her. She loved helping them, talking to them, handling their belly-warmed eggs while they watched on with big glassy eyes. They'd even nuzzle her hand with their beaks. Other, flightier ducks required great patience: she would quietly raise the walls a few stones each day, until they'd tolerate this new form of home. She took to carrying a rifle on her back, because the gulls and crows had learnt to follow her – a reliable guide to where they could find eggs to steal. The thieves had become fearless. The gun stopped that. It would have been far easier to protect the ducks if they'd nest closer to the sea barn, but they didn't.

~

She told me she had made a lot of mistakes, learning by trial and error, but she had learnt a great deal. The years came and went, and, glacially slowly, she had increased the number of nests on the outer islands and skerries. Then, at last, she got some ducks to nest on the main island itself. She longed to tell her father what she had done, but by then he didn't understand, and then, soon after, he died.

Anna wanted me to know how difficult it all was, and how much failure she had endured. Each spring she struggled to get the time off, and it was hard to juggle her home life with being away. Henning cared for the girls on Vega. He took them out to their mother on weekends, or in the holidays. Once, Anna's phone stopped working when she was out on the island, and he couldn't get hold of her to check she was OK. He was so worried that he sailed out and knocked on the door at 3 a.m., in the dark. It took her five years of hard work, with no pay, to get a single duck to nest on the main island. That Anna stuck with this slightly mad endeavour for so long took my breath away. It seemed obsessive and wildly stubborn. But Anna had seen the ducks accepting their nests on the skerries, and she seemed to have loved being out on the island so much she was prepared to wait, however long it took. Slowly, painfully slowly, she proved to everyone that her plan might actually be possible.

In the family album from those early years, there were a dozen pictures of Anna. She was the same age as I was now, almost fifty. In them, she is sitting in the sunshine on the decking in a T-shirt and shorts, lean, tanned, and barefoot, or in a rowing boat out on the water. She looks free.

~

From the moment *varntid* began, Anna spent most of her time in the living room. When she was tired she would nap on the sofa bed. She looked out of the windows a hundred times a day. The two rooms we lived in seemed to shrink when we could not leave them. I began to grow impatient with being indoors again for days and days.

Until, one morning, the wind dropped and the clouds started clearing. Anna said she felt in her bones that the ducks would come now. She went to the compost toilet and came back animated – she had seen some tell-tale white specks on the foreshore by Ship Island. It was starting.

On the bay and headlands, the ducks kept massing. They milled about looking bored, like unemployed workers in a film from the 1930s. They were finding their mates and plucking up the courage to come further onto the foreshore to choose nests. Or perhaps they were waiting for the weather to get warmer. The noises they made told Anna what they were up to. The males were reassuring their mates it was safe to keep going up the grass, encouraging them to be braver. They had a comic range of calls, which could be heard even when they couldn't be seen.

'Awhoa.'

'Awhoa.'

'Awhoa.'

And the females answered them. Anna said the female ducks were telling the males all the reasons why the nesting place might be dangerous, or the seaweed wasn't right. They sounded curiously like old married couples bickering.

~

That afternoon, a large male duck appeared near the house, proud and upright. His mate, Anna said, had gone into the wooden nest box near the barn. He filled my binoculars with his fine, wedge-shaped head. A band of black feathers widened from his yellowy-brown beak to the back of his head, and he had a rather chic velvety green patch running down his neck. He looked like he was wearing a cleopatra-style wig. The combination of this regal head and his pushed-out white chest made him appear pompous and self-important. But at least he had had the courage to come inland with his mate. Many of the other males just stood on the rocks and told their wives to go on ahead. Some managed to get to the shoreline, where they did a lot of rearing up and flapping of their wings. The brave male duck by the house peered around quizzically and chattered to himself. I was sorry to see him go when he waddled back to the shore.

There seemed to be far fewer female ducks than males. Perhaps this was because you could lose sight of a female eider on the foreshore from twenty feet away. Their brown feathers made them close to invisible unless they crossed a bright green patch of grass. Their dowdiness was, of course, a sensible evolutionary strategy. The males were here to show off, find a mate, impress her, impregnate her, offer a little moral encouragement as she found a nest, and then to go back to the sea to hang out with their friends. The males had evolved to be seen, to fuss, squabble, and fight.

The females had the much more dangerous work: going ashore, where no sensible duck wanted to be, finding a nesting place, making a nest, sitting patiently keeping eggs warm for twenty-eight days, and then taking their ducklings back to the sea across open ground. The ability to vanish into their surroundings was a way of staying alive in a place where almost every-thing would eat a duck. The female ducks evolved to be unseen.

~

The next day, huge, white, atomic clouds drifted across the ocean. There were perhaps fifty ducks now scattered round the shoreline. Some would wash themselves with a splash in the rockpools. We kept busy doing more house-hold repairs. Ingrid had a damp cloth and was rubbing marks from the paintwork. Anna tried to hang a cupboard in the kitchen. It was an old wooden box with no door and rusty hinges. She asked if it was level, and I said 'Not exactly,' and she laughed. I offered to hang it for her, and she said it was good to have a handyman around. She was in a wicked mood and told me her DIY work was shoddy. She said that a Russian woman would have hung the cup-board straighter for her man, and tried harder to please. Anna filled a box with teabags and other things that were cluttering her kitchen. She turned to Ingrid and said, 'I don't like men,' like it was the first time it had occurred to her. Ingrid laughed. 'We've known that for a while.'

Anna had a smile of pure mischief on her face. She told Ingrid exactly what she thought of men:

'They interfere and think they know best.'

Men, she said, wanted to come to the island and tell her what to do. They couldn't help it. They wanted women to do what they were told. And, when women refused, they went and got themselves a younger model. Someone who'd play the wife and smile at their jokes. But those Russian girls saw them coming. They fluttered their fake eyelashes and lay on their backs, and the men lost their heads and bought them a ring. But soon the housework went undone, and the end came fast. When the Russians left them, they took their money with them.

She said, 'You can put that in your story.'

Then she gave me a smile. 'If you ever think about having an affair, then I want you to ring me up and tell me.'

'What will you do?' I asked.

She laughed, and said, 'I will come to your house and . . .'

She said a word I didn't understand.

Ingrid translated: 'Throttle you.'

Ingrid and I were both laughing now. I promised I'd make the call if I ever felt weak.

'Maybe you will,' she said, 'but men are idiots.'

She was in full flow, the most animated I'd seen her. Men didn't like women working alone on the islands. They'd been programmed to think women needed them for everything. 'I don't need them,' she said, with some grit, 'and they know it.'

'They don't like the things I say, but you can't bottle everything up inside. If something needs saying, I say it, no matter what anyone thinks.'

Perhaps I should have felt offended for all the men on earth, but in truth I was delighted that Anna and Ingrid were now treating me as part of their sisterhood, someone they could say whatever they liked to.

I asked Anna how long she had been single, and she said nineteen years. She was standing on a chair filling a cupboard and declared that she still had 'admirers'.

'The trouble is, they aren't exactly top quality.'

They were, I learnt, all over eighty years old, and, as she put it, 'half dead'.

'I must be hot to really old guys,' Anna said. We were all now giggling like schoolgirls.

~

Later, Anna made supper. The light from the ocean glowed in the kitchen. Ingrid said her husband wanted a holiday, maybe somewhere in the sun, like Tenerife. Anna told her she shouldn't go. It would be packed with wrinkly old men pretending not to look through their sunglasses at twenty-year-old German girls in bikinis. She said she would be hot and clammy, like an aged walrus, in her swimsuit. And her skin would burn. Ingrid admitted she was not so keen on such holidays, but she would go.

Then, as if talking to herself, she said, 'We can't all just do what we want all the time. I come here each spring, this is my holiday. I come here, and he wants to go there, so I will go with him.'

~

Outside, more and more of the ducks were pairing up on the water. They hung together in the little bays. They were feeding in the inlet by the sea barn, ready for going ashore to find a nest. A female came up with a wriggling crab in her mouth. A huge, black-backed gull plunged down to grab it from her, and there was a splash as she dived to keep her dinner. The gull landed and floated on the surface, a little way away, waiting for another chance. The duck came back up and swallowed the crab quickly before the gull could even raise itself on its wings. The ducks paddled away and carried on feeding out in the channel.

Down on the foreshore beneath the house a dozen or so males could be seen. Most of them now had a wife by their side on the seaweed. Others idled, waiting for eligible feathered ladies to waddle around the headland. They bickered with one another about the females – and about their spots on the rocks. To intimidate, they lowered their heads and charged at each other, nipping their beaks. Sometimes there was a scuffle of wings and flashing feathers, a proper squabble.

We were surrounded by ducks now. We did our rounds slowly and quietly each day. If we let a duck-hut door click a little too loudly as we shut it, we'd see all the ducks inching away to the safety of the water.

~

I found myself thinking more and more about marriage. I had done something quite out of character, in leaving my wife and children far behind to come here. It felt selfish. I knew Helen was juggling everything at home, and must be overwhelmed holding it all together.

Anna had told me about the early days of her own marriages, and all about her children. I knew that she had split from Henning. But I was struggling to under-stand how anyone could let her go. She was magnetic. It was easy to imagine men falling in love with her; it was much harder to imagine someone choosing to give her up. I wondered what kind of husband I was, and whether I could screw it all up and lose Helen.

Helen loved me, but perhaps didn't always like me very much. She'd told me to take some time on the island to figure things out. I knew I'd helped make our life in many ways – we'd built a farmhouse, and fine flocks of sheep and a herd of cows, and I'd written books – but I was beginning to think I had been a little too much like Captain Ahab, a little too desperate to catch my whale, and everyone else had been dragged across the seven seas behind me.

There is a point where hard work and striving flips from something noble, making the lives of the people around you better, to something too intense, making their lives worse, and for a year or two I'd been on the wrong side of that line. I needed to listen more, slow down, and make space for Helen and my kids. I wanted to be a better version of me when I went home. I rang her and she laughed at my being schooled on a daily basis about the flaws of men by two militant Norwegian women. And I found myself fixating on the men in Anna's life and judging them harshly. I wondered if it was because I could see myself in them.

~

A few days later, I asked Anna about Henning. I wondered if her going out to the islands had contributed to their parting – had he felt forgotten about? And, for the first time, she snapped at me.

'I was married twice, and it ended twice. So what? I have four beautiful children from those marriages. It is enough.'

After the split, Anna moved out of the family home. Later, the roses she'd planted by the house blocked the drains with their tangled roots and caused no end of trouble. Anna laughed when she told me this, saying it was her slow revenge. She had got some money from her divorce. It wasn't enough, but she accepted it – she'd just wanted out.

She had no scores to settle, Anna said. She just got on with things, and, the following spring, she continued her island work. If she'd known she was going to be on her own, she might never have started to restore the duck station. The divorce – or 'Big Bang', as she called it – added a new layer of difficulty. But her brother helped her, just as he had done in school, when he'd protected her from bullies. They'd made the nests together, and he'd been a kind uncle to her girls. He'd chop logs, and repair and paint the buildings.

~

Just when it looked as though the ducks were going to come up to the nests, the wind got stronger. Ingrid gathered the washing on the line. Dark grey clouds blew in from the sea, and the light died on the waves. The shards of land visible from the windows were charcoal black. The tide raced in with the wind behind it. Waves crested white across the bay towards Flatholm. When we looked out at bedtime, the ducks had nearly all gone back to the water. They would not come ashore until this bad weather had passed. I lay in bed that night as the wind buffeted the roof – it sounded like I was lying under a sheet of tarpaulin. I wondered if it might undo our work, like the storm had in Anna's first season on Fjærøy. That would be a disaster: it was now too late to start again.

In the middle of the night, I woke up and looked out. Showers swept past. The luminous greens, yellows, whites, and blues had disappeared, replaced by monochrome grey, black, and white. The waves seemed to have carried the ducks out of the bay. The season had gone into reverse gear. I felt a stab of frustration.

~

After the stormy night, the island was strangely quiet. There were pairs of ducks everywhere out on the water, but they didn't seem in a hurry to come inland. That morning Anna said the ducks were wild, and would do whatever they decided to do.

Seeing I was crestfallen, she added, 'Don't worry, they will come back when it stops raining.'

We spent the morning collecting plastic rubbish from one of the inlets on the back of the island, which faced the ocean waves in winter. It was like the sea god had spewed up a stomachful of junk. Old fishing nets, plastic buoys, cyclists' drinking bottles, a broken blue fish box stamped 'BFP LIMITED LOWESTOFT', Coke bottles, plastic straws from fast food restaurants, lengths of plastic rope, shards of greenhouse plastic, big white fish trays washed overboard out at sea, roll-on deodorants, Head and Shoulders shampoo cartons, ear buds, flat and torn beach footballs, Evian bottles, and ready-salted crisp packets. The whole ravine was littered. We picked among the seaweed, filling green plastic bags. Ingrid sawed through a heavy white shipping rope, the thickness of her wrist, with a sharp knife. It came away and was tossed in a bag. Anna said she'd read in the newspaper that a submarine at the deepest part of the ocean found plastic on the seabed. We soon had several bags full, and Ingrid and I lugged them in stages up and across the rocks and back to the jetty. We heaped them up and laid logs on top to stop them blowing away until the conservation people came for them. Anna looked at Ingrid despairingly.

'It is everywhere . . . No wonder the young people are scared.'

~

The next day the gloomy weather passed on to the mainland, and the wind dropped. Anna fell asleep, and Ingrid ran a bucketful of water out of a little turn-tap on a 5-gallon plastic drum. Anna woke up and wanted to go out, but thought the sound of running water was me having a pee into a bucket in the porch (the drill if we could not leave the house for fear of disturbing ducks). She had politely ignored the sound for a minute or so, and then as the minutes passed had begun to wonder if I had a bladder problem. Eventually Ingrid returned and turned off the tap, and Anna realized the truth. When I got back from outside, five minutes later, the two women were in hysterics at Anna having waited for twenty minutes for me to stop urinating.

All day the ducks followed each other back round the headlands from the sea; this time they paddled in with real intent. Within a few hours, each rocky headland and section of shore was littered with white dots and companion brown dots – male and female eider ducks. And there were now lots more than before. Anna and Ingrid counted them excitedly from the windows or on their reconnaissance missions with binoculars across the headland. The ducks seemed eager to make up for lost time. There were too many to count. The males without partners tried to muscle in on the couples and had their tail feathers pulled or got chased across the water for their cheek. Everything about the sea estate had changed in a few short hours – the drabness and desolation of Fjærøyvær in its winter clothes already a fading memory.

Spring came with the ducks. Huge blue skies flooded with warm sunshine, punctuated only by the tiniest wisps of transparent cloud that layered backwards in a herring-bone pattern. From the top of Fjærøy, endless islands and skerries carved the water into a thousand silver-shining bays, pools, and channels. And, as the light changed, the vast coastline somehow moved closer, its jagged mountains and peaks wrapped around the little sea islands – a vast, encircling theatre of mountains, rocks, snow, islands, ocean, and light. Fjærøy was no longer a place on the edge of the world – it began to feel like the centre of the whole universe, everything revolving around its axis.

~

Anna watched the bay from her window. She slugged at a Coke bottle full of water.

'There are birds everywhere tonight,' she said, smiling. And I knew she meant not just that they were here, but they were coming to nest.

The females were already edging up the dusky shore. Soon there were ducks among the vegetation in front of the house. We peered out, watching for signs of ducks creeping to their nests, Ingrid at a bedroom window, me in the kitchen, and Anna kneeling on the sofa by her window. And we told each other what we saw, a running commentary as the hours passed.

From time to time, Anna quietly left the house for a better look. She trod slowly along the path to see what was happening. I followed. We'd keep moving until we felt seen, and then we'd freeze or retreat. The mother ducks would use every rock, hillock, and tussock of grass to get up the shore unseen. She said they often came in the half-light that passed for darkness here. Ingrid said she must get some sleep and went to bed. I stayed up another half an hour. I left Anna peeping through the window like a child trying to get a glimpse of Father Christmas.

~

I woke early. Ducks were calling to one another by the old cow byre. I went down to tell Anna. I opened the stiff living-room door quietly and saw her still by the window. She was dressed in blue-check pyjamas and a Shetland-style grey jumper. He hair fell loose to her shoulders. She looked a little boggle-eyed, like she had been out at a party, and I wondered if she'd been at this all night. She turned and smiled, and said quietly that she had been up for hours. She couldn't sleep. She looked younger, like when I had first met her. These ducks were everything to her. They were the magic of this place. Her strength returned with them. Their coming back seemed to vali-date all of her efforts over many years, and take away the fear that her last season would be a failure. She and the ducks were absolutely and mesmerizingly one thing, bound together. They were here because of Anna, coming back to their place of birth, where she had protected their mothers years earlier. Had their mothers told them that this human and this island could be trusted? That they must come back here and only here? Was it instinct? I wondered if the ducks ever saw her at the window, watching over them. I knelt on the sofa beside her. She pointed to a duck coming up to the barn and the little nest boxes, and whispered we must hold tight inside. It was easy to forget that these creatures, which seemed so homely waddling around the house, were wild seabirds.

After weeks of preparation, and long days of waiting, the first eiders had truly arrived. The relief in the house was palpable. It seemed miraculous that from across this vast, wild northern sea, these ducks had travelled to Anna's nests to lay their eggs.

I heard strange woodwind noises coming from under the floorboards. Anna held up a hand like we should not move an inch. A duck was chattering to herself eighteen inches beneath the sofa, perhaps to her mate outside in the grass, as she decided on a nesting place in the shadows beneath the house.

Ingrid appeared with bed-hair, looking tired. She pointed to the floor as a question and we both held our fingers to our lips and smiled. After a while, Anna told us that the duck beneath the house had slipped out and away, through the green clumps of water marigolds, and to the sea. The laying had begun.

5.

The Ducks

Anna is lying on her belly in the shadows under the floor of the red-painted barn, a few metres from the house. She crawls forward on the black dust. All around her are nests we made a week or so ago. The only light flows in through a small pop-hole cut for the ducks. I squeeze in beside her, keeping my head down so as not to crack it on the timber floor joists. I notice, with some nervousness, that the whole chunky barn is propped up by just a few stones stacked on top of each other. If it were to slip off the stones, we would be flattened. There are no ducks on the nests, but Anna thinks they have been here. Maybe she's seen their marks in the dust, or noticed the seaweed has been disturbed. She rummages knowingly in the loose ground, and then her fingers find what they are searching for. She says, 'Ah,' and smiles, pulling from deep in the floor the most beautiful egg I have ever seen. It fills her small palm. In my hand, it feels waxy and thick-shelled. This oval lump of green pottery is maybe twice as heavy as a hen's egg, and has a more pronounced cone-like end. This is the first egg we have found. Anna tells me that we must keep an eye on this place, and not kneel on it in the days that follow. If the duck prefers to lay in the dust, rather than in one of our beautiful nests, then so be it. She will at least be safe in here.

~

These jewels were soon appearing in nests all over the island. We had two responsibilities now. The first was the same as before: to be quiet. The second was to inspect every nest each morning, and count the growing clutches of eggs.

I had imagined the ducks would commit to the nests – and would sit on them – from the first visit, slowly adding to their clutch. But the first few eggs laid, Anna explained, were hidden by the duck. She would come up to the nest, lay an egg, and then go back to the shoreline before morning. This was repeated every night until she had a full clutch buried under the seaweed. When the nest was full, she would sit and brood them. For that first week or so of laying, the nests rarely had a duck on them – just another egg left each morning, and a warmth betraying the bird that had just ghosted away.

Our daily inspections would continue for weeks, until we reached high summer, because the last birds would come to lay nearly a month after the first. We would go out each morning after breakfast, once Anna had judged the ducks were calm on their nests or back safely on the sea.

We saw very few ducks up close in the first week. They watched their nesting places from the water, sometimes a quarter of a mile away.

Anna never rushed, but she was highly efficient. No movement was wasted. She'd hum gently as she approached the hut doors to let the ducks know she was coming. Then, carefully, she would peer in. If all was quiet inside, she'd open the door, crawl in, and touch and lift the seaweed swirls to see if any eggs had been laid. Once she had seen everything of interest, she would silently close the door and move on. For several hours a day Anna and Ingrid would now be opening hut and nest-box doors, peering in, or climbing in and fiddling, judging, and then closing the doors.

The three of us worked around the island, slowly leapfrogging each other to the next nest in need of work. Anna made me shadow her until she was satisfied I had learnt how to do the task carefully, with enough attention on the ducks on the water. She taught me to be aware of the ducks all around the headlands and on the sea – their noises and movement were a simple indicator of the stress we were causing the birds, and we had to adjust our work to account for that. If they raised their heads they were anxious about our approach, and their mates on the water made strange woodwind-sounding 'oohs' and 'aahs', as if warning each other. If they waddled to the water we had disturbed them, and if they took flight and flapped and splashed across the waves we had made a big mistake, and Anna would be cross.

I wore the same clothes for several days, and, when I joked about having fleas, she said it was OK. She wore the same old trousers so there were no new smells to scare the birds. The ducks got used to the same people, she said, and would begin to trust us. After an hour of this work we would head back to the house, having inspected perhaps a third of the island. Each day, it would take two or three expeditions, broken up by coffee and dinner breaks, to get round the main island and the islets we could walk to. Sometimes Ingrid would wander off and we would see her, later on, far across the rocks on Crow Island, checking nests for eggs. We went to the other islands with nests much less often, and only when the sea was calm.

~

After a week or so of coming ashore, the birds would relax, their bond to the land and their nests growing stronger. We were then able to spend greater stretches of time outside without scaring them. It was mid-May and the days were growing longer and warmer. In the afternoons we would sit on the deckchairs, drinking black coffee and talking quietly about nothing in particular. We became obsessed with the happenings on Ship Island, two hundred feet from the house. We watched the tides rise and fall around that special little islet day after day. A drake waddled up the rocks there, followed by two females. He seemed full of bravado and giddy with excitement. His chest was puffed out, and he was stiff upright, leading the way. The female ducks were more tentative, like first-time buyers viewing a potential property. Anna thought she saw one of the females crawl into a stone nest.

The ocean rippled back into the bays and inlets, until the whole seascape looked like a saucer full beyond the rim with water. Ducks clustered on the shrinking rocks. Others paddled across the large rock pools. Anna rolled up her trouser-legs and sleeves and, leaning backwards, closed her eyes and soaked up the sunshine. She looked healthier, and every day she walked further and worked for longer.

I had begun to wonder if Anna was really going to stop after this season. I sensed that Ingrid wanted to know, too, but didn't dare ask. Ingrid went to the kitchen to bring us all some yoghurt and muesli, so I asked Anna if she'd ever stop coming here. She opened her eyes, but didn't seem to hear me, and instead looked out across the sea.

~

One morning we entered the old cow byre to find a duck sitting calmly on its nest. Anna nudged me in the ribs. She was grinning from ear to ear. She edged in quietly and crawled across the floor, making gentle reassuring noises to the bird, 'Oye, oye, la, la, la.'

Anna felt beneath the duck and said she had six eggs. The duck looked at her with what I thought was wry amusement. I was surprised she was so placid. Until now we'd only seen the ducks out in the open, where they would flap away at the very sight of us. On the nest, Anna whispered, they had a quite different nature. They were practically glued down, and would hold still so Anna could touch the eggs under their bellies. Only a handful were nervous and wild-eyed; Anna would approach those incredibly slowly, or simply back away.

Lining the nest of that first bird we came across, I could see a circle of light-grey eiderdown, which the duck had plucked from her chest with her beak. The perfect bedding material. In the days that followed, this duck, and every other that sat on a nest, would pull more and more from their chests, until they sank into its softness. Anna told me that in cold years the nests would have more down, as the birds did whatever it took to keep their eggs warm. This grey cloud of fluff was the reason for all our work – the basis of a whole way of life.

I asked Anna if it was the eiderdown or the ducks that she loved, as technically we were here for a harvest. She said it was the ducks, like that was a stupid question. I should have known the answer. She smiled like a child as she handled that first duck, as though she was the loveliest, most magical being in all creation.

Only the elation of lambing time, when every moment is charged with purpose, felt comparable to what I was experiencing now. When new life, and sometimes death, is all around you, adrenaline pumps through your veins. If the whole world beyond this island had ceased to exist, I am not sure we would have noticed. At the end of each day we would get back to the house and slump into our chairs. Though I felt exhausted, I was also elated, because I knew Anna had recovered. Deep inside, I had known she would. She was as hard as the rocks beneath our feet. It wasn't just that she was back working. It was that her self-belief was back. She was the engine of this place, of our tiny community. I needed to get that defiance back in myself. Being with Anna, here, was recharging my batteries to go back and fight my own battles, and do better at home. I could feel some of that spirit rising in me again.

~

Every day Anna would teach me something. There were quirks and details about her work that were entirely alien and fascinating. She always carried a drawstring bag on her tours of the nests, and I soon became familiar with its contents. When she suspected a nest had been used overnight, she'd feel into it with her hand for the looseness or warmth that confirmed her hunch. More often than not, there would be an egg buried an inch or two down. The first egg in a nest, Anna explained, was the rent egg – earmarked for the island owner – and it was our job to store it safely back in the house, ready for collection.

To make sure the bird didn't discover this theft and abandon the nest, Anna replaced it with a carved wooden egg, or dummy egg. The dummy eggs also helped fool the herons, ravens, and crows. They were clever enough to raid the nests, but if they found a wooden egg, they'd throw it away in disgust and not return to be tricked twice.

The ducks mostly ignored the dummy egg, or accepted it as the one they'd left in the dark the night before. Some older ducks nudged them out of the nest when they had real eggs safely beneath them. Anna thought the ducks had worked out themselves a long time ago that having a decoy in the nests frustrated and confused predators. They sometimes pulled almost-egg-sized human junk, like lightbulbs or jam jars, into their nests.

Some of Anna's dummy eggs were just sanded drift-wood, but they would easily pass for a real egg in the depth of the seaweed. Others were more beautiful, painted blue or green, with a bold 'A' for Anna carved on one side. Anna's neighbour on Vega made these in his barn through the winter. They had a five-inch length of string tacked to their bottom, at the end of which hung a little wooden peg. Anna set them in the nests, carefully burying the orange string and anchoring the peg under the edge. Some were worn smooth from years of rough hands, coarse seaweed, and duck beaks and feet. In the log shed there were others, made of plastic – these were the least used of all. Someone had bought them in the past, but they weren't as good, and most were cracked and broken.

Anna's drawstring bag also held a bundle of rubber gloves – not for wearing, but used like sleeping bags for the rent eggs. Anna would slip each egg into the palm of a glove, bloating it like a swollen dead frog, though the fingers stayed empty. The gloves stopped the eggs from cracking against each other in the bag as she walked. When Anna got back to the house after each nest-inspecting trip, she carefully peeled off the gloves and stacked the eggs in a milk-bottle crate in the pantry. The crate of eggs filled each day, beneath the shelves packed with flour, baked beans, and bags of muesli.

Anna always looked pained when she took the first egg. She didn't like taking them, but said it was for the best. A duck had no chance in Fjærøy with a giant brood of ducklings – a smaller brood could get away to sea. Terje took thirty eider eggs in rent each season, and Anna's predecessor, the duck woman here before her, was entitled to twenty. So fifty eggs were due in obligations. Anna told me that when she retired she would not claim any eggs. The birds could keep them and take their chances.

~

The island was so calming because its routines were simple and repetitive. Each day we went out on our nest inspections. Anna would start by quietly lifting the panels away and climbing underneath the house. Ingrid would take me to check all the nests on the southern and western sides of the island. Then we'd meet back up and swap notes. When one of us found a new egg we'd report back breathlessly. Hour after hour passed like this, and it was often late afternoon before we'd checked the whole main island. Anna trusted me to inspect the nests among the rocks and ravines that she found hard to get to, but hung on my every word about what I saw. The sun shone. We sailed on Anna's elation, and the house was buzzing with every duck seen coming inland, or every new egg found.

The cherries had rotted in a bag in the pantry and I threw them onto the compost heap, where the fieldfares pecked at them. When they fluttered out to the rocks, tails raised, they made a noise like someone swinging a plastic rattle. I peered into the gooseberry bush and spied their nest – a perfect bowl woven with dried grass. I checked it each morning after that and saw it filling with tiny, pale blue eggs.

Once, during this morning ritual, I heard a scuffling further on, beneath the bushes. Scratching and cooing. I bent back the branches and saw three ducks sitting in scrapes in the ground covered with a few twigs and litter. The ducks often found their own nesting places, as they would in the wild, and they liked this hidden place. They'd be relatively safe there – but it was a nuisance cleaning the down from such dirty ground nests.

Next to the gooseberry bushes, in this old kitchen garden, was the potato patch, and lots of smaller nest boxes made from wood and corrugated tin, or old 45-gallon fuel drums with the ends cut off. Most of these were still empty, but Anna checked them daily, peering into the knee-high clumps of nettles and delphiniums. One morning, she looked under the redcurrant bushes, a place she hadn't looked before, and found a nest with five eggs in it. She told us about this nest with a dead rat hanging limp from a trap in her hand. The rat was pregnant, swollen bellied. They would eat the potatoes from under the ground if she didn't kill them. She took the rat to the foreshore and dropped it from the trap. A low droning sound came from far away, back towards the mainland. Military aircraft, Ingrid said.

~

Anna sat at the dining table and wrote up the nest notes. An ornate and unused oil lamp hung above her from the ceiling, and biros lay scattered by her hand. A glass vase of sea-eagle feathers, quills almost as thick as her fingers, sat on the table next to her. Hanging from the tongue-and-grooved, white-painted walls were portraits of the owner's ancestors. Sea captains and their elegant wives, elderly couples in their Sunday best, and old fishermen in thick woollen jumpers. A little blond boy and a girl peek in from the side of one photo, as if looking into the future.

A ring folder was left open on the table. A ledger recording which nest boxes were being used, and how many eggs were in each. And next to it a diary, where Anna was scribbling down the work we'd done.

She got paid a small stipend from the authorities

to do the duck work, and they asked that she keep records.

Brass-band marching music played on the radio. The bay by the sea barn was luminous turquoise. Tern Island glowed lime green, and the rocks shone black. The battle between sea and land had turned in land's favour. The island was now blanketed with vegetation that muffled the sea and wind.

As I passed over the hill one morning, I heard piping noises all around. I looked up and the sky was full of golden plovers suspended, almost hovering, on the sea wind. I wished them well on their journey north.

~

Beneath the red barn there now sat the most elegant of mother ducks. We had seen her go in, and had heard her laying. And now she watched as Anna crawled in the shadows to inspect the nests around her. The bird gently pecked at her hand when she got too close. Anna murmured to her, 'Don't worry . . . You are beautiful . . . I will not hurt you.'

The duck curled its neck submissively onto its own back. It reminded me of the way my grandfather's horses had looked at him, with big, trusting eyes, as he felt down their legs in the stables. People get lost in such craft for decades, in the skill, intimacy, and thoughtfulness it requires, the work becoming its own reward. Anna must have loved this work, and the ducks, because she hadn't earned a penny from doing it for several years, when she began. I'd done the same for many years, working on the farm without taking any wages, and, like her, doing other half-hated jobs to pay the bills. I asked whether she had been recognized for what she was trying to do, but Anna said her work on Måsøy went largely unremarked-on by anyone outside her family. For years no one else much knew or cared what she was up to. And yet, what she was doing was remarkable. It had probably been a thousand years, or more, since anybody had succeeded in an undertaking like it. It was true that experienced duck people had long known you could house a wild duck if you were careful and quiet – they did it with birds that came to their islands and nested outside on the ground, to add to their stock of ducks. But no one on this coastline had re-established a whole island of nests in a place that the ducks had abandoned and mistrusted.

~

As more and more ducks colonized our island, they animated the whole place. One day I went to the outhouse and met a pair of ducks coming up the path towards me. I reversed, stepping up the bank several strides to clear the path, and then stood as they waddled past me. The female made a grumpy quacking in my direction, like I had no business there.

The first week or so, the birds had mainly been interested in the old nesting huts down by the wharf, so these had multiple occupied nests in them, and were the most exciting spots to inspect each morning. But soon they started laying in nests in the other, more remote places, like the huts on Crow Island and in the Summer Barn at the top of the hill.

Ten days in, Anna told us we were up to eighty-three nesting birds. She was thrilled: it was an impressive score for this early in the season. But you had to be paying attention to enjoy this shy spectacle. Many of the ducks were making their journeys and laying in the early hours, others were now tucked away in their shadowy places, all over the sea estate.

Still, that night she began to fret for the birds that were sitting on nests. They seemed untroubled to me, but she knew better. The next morning, we found a pile of feathers and some cold eggs in a hollow on the hillside. Anna said the duck had been killed – this was all that was left. We had been served notice: whatever the predator turned out to be, it would likely come back. Later that day a sea eagle sat on one of the stone duck houses on Ship Island. Ingrid feared for the duck in it, but, when she got there, the eagle had flown away and the mother duck was sitting quite calm, stuck on her nest, just a few inches below the roof where the eagle's talons had been.

The next day, Anna found a duck had laid in the open, in a shadowy ravine that ran between the main island and North Rock. The duck was in the bay watching us. Anna said her eggs would be taken by a gull unless we built a shelter around them. We would have to build it in two stages so as not to alarm the mother. She would come the first night and suffer the half-built walls that had appeared round her eggs, and the next day we would add a roof and hope she was brave enough to climb in again.

The pile of feathers and the duck laying in the open changed the mood. Anna said we must watch more carefully. We searched for eggs in every nook and cranny on the island, every crack and fissure in the foreshore. Either we found them, or other beady eyes would.

~

The buds on the peony were filling now, like tight green scoops of ice cream with a hint of raspberry peeking out. The wind knotted the tea towels on the washing line as Anna gathered them in. In the distance, the Arctic terns screeched and cried. The upper foreshore was now embroidered with colourful little flowers. And lower down, among the rocks, the roseroot had its moment, its yellows and brilliant chalky green soon dissolving away into rusty clumps that dropped back, spent, in the race for the sky. After checking the nests on the neighbouring islets, I gathered driftwood for future nest-repairs.

The male ducks formed rafts in the bays. Some came in close, out of the rising wind. Two fought and splashed in the rock pool between the house and Ship Island, frothing the water, until the winner pulled the tail feathers of the loser and bullied him back to the bay. Two snipe chased each other round the island erratically, like bits of shrapnel blown end over end through the sky, their oboe-like call surrounding us. Anna kept an eye on the ducks by the shore. A female goosander stood on a rock on the hill behind the house, angular and alert. They loved to nest under the nest boxes, like squatters. Their pinky-cream eggs had no value to her, but I sensed she enjoyed having them in the huts.

~

New ducks were still coming ashore, at a rate of seven or eight or more a day. The numbers were looking better and better in Anna's nest diary. It felt like the colony might rise to match the old days. Anna said there was no way of knowing when they would stop coming ashore, but I think she was excited and hopeful too.

She told me someone would read the nest reports back at the museum, maybe the seabird scientists. But there seemed a vast distance between the simple words she wrote down,

Wednesday, 18th May: Crow Island — old stone house with opening towards Flatholm. First egg taken by the crow.

and the epic life she lived each spring. These first weeks of nesting, as the ducks were coming ashore and gathering around the house, made Anna seem almost mystical. It was like she had somehow called them in from the open ocean to her voice and her gentle, stroking hands. The ducks seemed enchanted by her, unafraid.

~

We discovered a duck nesting down by the jetty, under the wooden walkway, blithely ignoring us tramping over it just inches above its head. Another had nested next to the house, two feet from the path, in the lush grass. Anna said she had done the same the previous year. There was no need to build huts around all of these ducks now, she told us, as the rising vegetation would hide them.

Another bird had nested in a depression in the rocks, relying entirely on her camouflage. We almost stepped on her. 'Oh, hello,' said Ingrid. I found another nest in one of the huts at the top of the island with two eggs in it, which told us we had missed the nest the day before. Ingrid said it was a miracle, because she had knelt on that ground and somehow not smashed the hidden egg. Anna had once trodden on a hidden nest and broken all the eggs inside.

The island was now a chaotic mass of nests and tangled routes to and from the sea. Anna's head was full of every minute detail of it. Ingrid and I kept up as best we could.

The three of us walked up the grassy hill. Thirty feet behind us, a duck waddled along the path. We stood in the doorway of the log shed. The duck came to the red barn called Buret, with its worn wooden steps, then turned up past the compost heap, through the yellow celandines, to the fruit bushes. There was a rustling of leaves and twigs. Anna was beaming. She whispered to me, 'That duck has come back to the same spot for many years. She has been on this island longer than me.'

~

Each of those Arctic summer days felt like a lifetime of light. Anna spent the hottest days in her plastic sunlounger on the decking, behind the white picket fence at the end of the house. The whole ocean played out before her, and she became lost in it. She delighted in little things. The ducks drifting back into the inlet. The noisy brown redshanks fighting and racing each other around the barns. The bumble bee that landed on the decking, exhausted, and which she revived with some honey on a spoon.

If she was not watching, she was listening, because half the experience of the islands was heard. The wind brought the raucous sound of the gull colony from the north. A pair of starlings raced to and fro between their feeding ground on the meadow and their nest in the eaves above. They squeezed through a hole, and scratled into the nest. The chicks screeched for food. When the mother bird left the nest, a small wisp of eiderdown fell and landed on the table next to Anna's wrinkled hand.

The duck beneath the fruit bush was quacking quietly. 'She is having her egg,' she said.

A large, white cruise ship appeared by Vega, and caught a ray of sunshine. The two women peered at it through their binoculars. They found the tourists amusing, because they went to Vega, the tamest of places, but were nervous like they were visiting an Arctic wilderness and might see a polar bear.

Ingrid and Anna both had increasingly sun-bleached hair, and the ruddy, tanned cheeks that all Norwegians had in the old photos. Anna had filled out a little and looked younger, and the make-up she'd worn in the first few weeks had disappeared.

~

Whenever life was starting to feel too easy, Fjærøy had a habit of reminding you that it was a wild place. Anna was sitting at the table outside when specks of rain landed on its laminated surface. The edges of the table were curled upwards from previous soakings. The sky darkened. Grey clouds slowly smothered the sun. Anna collected her jumper, shoes, and an empty mug from the top of the fence and carried them inside. A starling croaked and whistled on the rocks behind the house. Rain showers passed across the ocean to the south.

Fat drops of rain sploshed down on the worn, sunbleached decking. The mainland was lost in the gloom, and the island felt lonelier.

Ingrid lit the stove and turned on the radio. The rain was hammering at the window and the gutters soon echoed with the downpour. The sea's grey acres soon blurred into the sky.

The rain set in, flowing down the windows hour after hour. The women sat on the sofa talking. The mother ducks were almost all settled on their nests, where they were safely sheltered.

Anna wound wool around the back of the armchair, and then into a ball in her hands, winding and winding, until the ball was as big as a cabbage. She untangled knots as she went. Ingrid was knitting another pair of socks from a ball of grey wool I had brought as a gift.

The wind blew all night. The rain beat on the corrugated tin roofs of the duck huts as we looked for eggs the next morning. Anna saw that a crow had stolen an egg, and the mother duck had shit everywhere and abandoned her nest. The shitting, she said, was an old wild trick to make the remaining eggs less appealing to thieves. We paused in a hut, escaping the worst of the rain. The clouds to the north had dropped to the sea. 'It is raining on my house,' Ingrid said when we got back inside. She was looking at the white wall of her house on Vega with the binoculars. I wondered if she felt homesick. The sea between her and home was a deep blue, broken only by cresting waves that rose up like horses.

After the long days of sunshine and watching the world change, the rainy days inside were doubly boring. As if guessing my thoughts, Anna said islands were not holiday resorts. In his later years, if he heard anybody romanticizing island life, her father would stop them, telling them that the people out there worked from morning to night. That fishing life was brutal. He said he had got sick of goose sausages, seal, and porpoise. He told his kids that he didn't want to eat any more cormorant this side of the grave – his mother had made meatballs out of them.

The bad weather went on for three days. The light had a strange luminescent quality. The wind battered the island, its every gust carrying on up from the foreshore and through the rustling grass.

The work didn't stop. Each morning we did the rounds, cursing quietly at the mud in low places and the seaweed in the nests going mouldy-white at the edges. Then we would go inside to dry out.

Ingrid was busy chopping vegetables, Anna updating her nest diary. I went to the log shed for wood for the stove; the rain was cold on my neck as I opened the rusty catch. I could hear through the rain the ducks on their nests chatting: sharp consonants, and oohs of surprise, and gentle questions, and beaks clacking like knitting needles.

Later, from the living-room window, we could see the clouds, like triffids, walking across the ocean on columns of grey rain. 'The Girl from Ipanema' played on the radio. Ingrid poured us another cup of coffee.

~

By evening, the rain had stopped. Anna had been knitting for hours, watching through the window. Suddenly, she stiffened and said, 'A thief.'

She dropped her wool and needles and rushed for the door. We followed. Anna was out on the decking, staring hard at a point in the sky over Ship Island. There was an Arctic skua sailing up and down the wind. It was blacker than black against the grey. Its wings were like two Zs hinged on one end, tumbling through the sky. It lowered above the mounds on Ship Island, like it knew eggs or ducklings were hidden below. Anna nodded to the porch and I knew what she wanted. The rifle.

The skua had the strange effect of silencing all the other birds. They seemed to know something savage had come among them. Ingrid dashed down the grass, waving her arms, fifty metres away. The skua seemed quite unafraid, as though it knew that the tide separated us from the nests, and that this woman was too old to swim. She turned back towards Anna in horror. Skuas were terrible thieves. It would pull the nest out and gobble up the eggs. Anna looked at me and said, 'Shoot it.' I slid the bullet in with a tiny click and cocked it shut, all the time watching the skua. I raised the gun to my shoulder and prepared for the crack of the shot.

But the skua took one look at me with the rifle, turned down the wind, and flew effortlessly away. It was soon at the gull colony to the north, which erupted in noise. I relaxed and lowered the gun. Anna nodded and returned to the house. She was not at all sentimental about death;

she had meant I should kill the skua, and, had it hesitated a moment longer, I would have.

The little brown birds on the barn roof with the red legs started piping again, and then chased each other playfully across the hillside.

~

Later that evening, in the ghostly twilight, Ingrid came across the headland with a strange wooden crucifix draped across her shoulder. When she stood it upright, it became a scarecrow, with a fisherman's coat falling from its cross-rail. A smirking face was scrawled on a deflated old football and stuffed on the top. Anna said it would scare the predators away, and I agreed it definitely would, provided they were familiar with 1970s horror movies.

~

The next day the barometer by the bookshelf said the weather was shifting for the better. Anna hoped that still more ducks would come and nest. We went out to see if any were around.

A sea of whispering grass now grew on the hillside round the old engine and pump. Beyond that, half-grown clumps of meadowsweet filled the air with an almond smell when we brushed through them. The day was brightening; the island's plants were racing for the sky, using every ray of sunlight in this short northern summer.

The rain had ruined a few of the empty nests. We rebuilt the ones that had been most spoiled with dry seaweed that was stored in the barn.

~

The barn that Lars had repaired looked naked without a coat of paint. So, one day, when the ducks seemed settled, I took the tin, a brush, and a screwdriver and headed down the grass path. I levered off the stiff lid with the screwdriver and swirled the Falun-red paint with a stick. I stood on a pallet and boxes to paint the highest parts.

Anna came and grumbled gently about Lars not having done the work quite how she intended. She helped me paint, offering up a running commentary on the ducks paddling shyly back into the bay, and the geese grazing beyond that on Tern Island. The male eider ducks sailed past us in the inlet, huffing and puffing.

Another male duck watched like a sentry from the inlet by the boathouse. He called gently to his mate sitting on the nest. Anna made the noise back to him:

'Awhooa.'

'Awhooa.'

She giggled and said, 'They talk to each other like man and wife.'

Later, Ingrid called to us that supper was ready. When

we walked down the path on the way back to the house, one of the drakes was standing idly on the headland. Another saw us and rose from a nearby rockpool, clattering across the surface and away across the bay to feed. Days later, the redshanks, little brown waders with red legs, had christened the new barn paint with splatters of white shit on the window ledge.

~

I noticed that, for all she paid attention to the sea and the birds, Anna still followed whatever gossip there was to be gleaned from Ingrid's phone calls home, or from her own occasional calls with Terje. The successes and failures of the other duck stations travelled on these winds. 'They say they have three hundred sitting on nests on Flatholm,' Ingrid said, after one such phone call. Anna said, caustically, that they must double-count their nests. I said that she was competitive, like I was with my flock at home, and Anna said the numbers mattered.

It seemed that if we got more than a hundred nests to harvest we would avoid failure, and we had passed that now. More might still come, but even if they didn't, we had done OK. Our ducks now spent their days sitting and pulling down from their chests. We'd peer in at them, and often touch them gently, and, as we passed round the island, we began to see tiny grey escaped feathers blowing around, tumbling across the grass. There were still female eiders milling about on the open water. I watched them silently, willing them to find a mate and come ashore whilst there was still time.

~

The male ducks mostly drifted away to sea once their mates were settled on the nests. The last gang of them gathered idly on the headlands for a day or two, then vanished overnight. Eventually, there were only two left – two black-and-white specks on the foreshore. The island became much quieter. The duck bickering and calling ceased. The water was still.

I asked Anna where they'd gone, and she schooled me. The males soon moult their flight feathers and cannot fly, so they hang out in big crowds far out on the ocean. The females moult later, when the work is done with their ducklings.

'I am always sad when they leave,' Ingrid told me, quietly. 'The island feels greyer and somehow lonelier without them.'

~

One afternoon it was not quite warm enough to sit outside, so Anna and Ingrid knitted and watched the sea from their window. Anna sent me to turn on the generator so she could bake bread, and she put on the old TV.

Anna saw something and darted out of the house.

Ingrid and I followed her through the kitchen. On the way to the door I lifted the rifle from its corner. Another raid.

Three sea eagles were landing on Ship Island near the eider nests.

Anna was clapping her hands out on the decking, and Ingrid had grabbed two pan lids that she bashed together above her head. They were going crazy, banging and yelling, desperate – the nests on Ship Island were almost sacred. I could see the fear in Anna's eyes. If we couldn't protect the nests right on our doorstep, what was the point of us being there?

I looked down the sight of the rifle. I felt uncomfortable, unsure if shooting a sea eagle was a jailable offence, but ready to murder if Anna told me to.

Thankfully, the eagles were rattled by the two lunatic women yelling at them and sloped off to sit sulkily on the tidal-marker poles half a mile away. A raven passed over idly and was given the banging-pans treatment too: it got a shock and tumbled as though it had been attacked by a peregrine, then recovered its dignity and headed away.

Later, when the tide allowed, we went across to Ship Island and peered through the wooden holes, making sure the eider ducks were OK. I caught glimpses of mottled feathers, and the profiles of proud ducks safely tucked in the shadows.

~

The island was now a city of nests, all at different stages of laying and incubating. We checked each one almost every day, coming back with our news for Anna and her nest diary.

A new duck sitting under the barn.

A first egg laid in a nest on Crow Island, in the boxes.

A second egg laid in the box by the potato patch.

When Anna went out, it was mesmerizing to watch her working on the rocks, from hut to hut, and insanely beautiful at times. Rarely have I seen anyone so absorbed in each living moment. I began to understand the old Norwegian myths about the rocks and mountains coming alive, shapeshifting into creatures that were half human and half geology. This way of living demanded a loss of self, a surrendering to the rocks, rain, wind, and tides. I was coming to see that those tales were about the people themselves.

Anna saw things that Ingrid and I could not see – could spot emerging problems that needed solutions. One day she noticed a nesting duck that was taking too frequent trips to bathe in the sea. I was in awe that, out of the many dozens of birds sitting and going to and from the water every day, she noticed this one's strange bathing habits. We went down to the nest and found it infested with red mites. Every time the bird went into the sea to wash them off, she came back wet, and the nest was damp as a result. The damper it got, the more mites there would be, until she would perhaps abandon her clutch. Anna and I cleaned away the mouldy old nest, laid down a square of plyboard for a base, and made it afresh with dry seaweed. The eggs would not rot now. Anna feared the duck would abandon the new nest, but she was sensible and came back.

~

The gooseberry bushes were now humming with insects. Their tiny flowers, hanging beneath the leaves, buzzed with bumble bees. The peonies opened in the old garden, with big, blousy red petals. As the light stretched deeper and deeper into what once had been night, time became meaningless. We took lunch when we felt like it, 3 p.m. on some days, the simplest of meals, yoghurt and muesli with sliced banana on top or a bowl of porridge. Anna took a nap in the afternoons, and sometimes Ingrid did too. And I would read. It might be 5 p.m. before we went out again after lunch. No one worried about an evening meal until 8 p.m. or so. By nine at night it was cooler, and we lit the fire in the stove in the living room and ate crisps with garlic paste. Anna occasionally pulled the starter cord on the generator, firing it to life to put the cold back in the old fridge. The TV blared out news about a Norwegian princess falling in love with a shaman. A priest said it was a scandal, and Anna got angry at the screen, like she couldn't believe anyone cared about this nonsense. Sometimes we ate boiled eider eggs from the rent-eggs stash in the pantry, peeling off their thick, concrete-like shells. The yolk was a deep orange, and they tasted a little fishy.

~

Anna came back from one of her rounds excited. She had found a nest in the old cow byre where broken shells told her the eggs had hatched. She took me to see the ducklings peeping out from beneath the mother's wing. Tiny little two-tone brown balls of fluff, with smooth, grey beaks and comically over-sized sea feet.

The mother sat quiet and didn't seem alarmed at our presence. Anna lifted one of the tiny birds in her hands and held it up. It cheeped and raised its head like it might topple from her grasp, so she cupped it more closely.

Anna put the duckling back beneath its mother's belly and said to her, 'Now you must take them back to the sea . . . and avoid those gulls.'

~

All that was left of the nest, when we checked it the next morning, was the eiderdown. It was just lying there, like an afterthought, the nest-rent paid. The down tingled in our fingers, fluffy, clean, and dry, almost weightless.

Gathering and cleaning the eiderdown left behind in

the hatched nests would be the next big task – the work that would take us to the end of our island days.

This stage of the season passed quickly. A brood of ducklings hatched over a day or so, and then gathered their strength, went down behind their mother to the sea, and were gone. Often, we'd miss it altogether, finding only the broken eggshells or chicks' membranes, and an empty crown of seaweed and down. No thank you, no drama, just a quiet slipping away. After all the work we'd put in to make it happen, it was hard not to feel short-changed.

No two nests harvested the same. Some were glorious and clean and bulky – like two or three might fill a cushion. It was easy to see the eiderdown from the cleanest nests being valuable – it looked luxurious, and it was mesmerizingly light and soft to touch. The down seemed grey in the shadows, but, carried out into the daylight, it became speckled, because the tiny feathers were white nearest to the quill.

In some nests we'd find just a small handful of down. In others, the down looked worthless: tangled with seaweed stems, or dirt and sticks, or – worse – damp and covered in shit. A lot of work would follow, to rescue the value from these poorer bundles.

Though this harvest was precious, and I marvelled at the strange, almost weightless bundles of expensive fluff, I could see that, for Anna, each empty nest was a light going out – a moment of sadness. She was happy the ducklings had gone to the sea, happy we had some down, but mostly she seemed wistful that the life-force of that nest, which had been so thrilling and so personal to her, was now gone. I saw then that Anna empathized with the ducks as a mother. She understood the sacrifice they were making, understood they would risk every-thing for their young.

The spirit was draining out of the island, one duck and her family at a time. Anna treasured any sighting of a brood leaving, either passing through the vegetation or getting to the waves and bobbing away with their moth-ers, out on the channel.

~

Despite the wild and hard nature of these islands, Fjærøy was a place of kindness and warmth: a nursery. I had been so busy admiring Anna's toughness that I had missed something simpler – she was a mum and a carer. She knew all about living on an island in a wooden house, being a single mother, and making it work, however big the challenges. She identified with the ducks she worked hard to protect.

~

I began to watch and listen carefully to how Anna and Ingrid spoke to each other, and saw how different it was to the way the men who had visited spoke and behaved.

Because I hadn't wanted to spoil their dynamic, I had sensed I ought to make myself much smaller when I arrived on the island, working to their commands, relinquishing responsibility. I had rarely done anything like it before. It wasn't just that we were removed from the noise of the modern world – for the first time in my life, I realized, I was in a place entirely run by women. By paying attention, I began to see what men and women do to one another, how we trap ourselves, and each other, in certain roles. And the truth is, it was embarrassing to see it clearly for the first time. When I remembered how the men spoke over Anna, or assumed she needed them to do things for her, I cringed inside, because I knew I must do those things too.

~

As the nests emptied, Anna, Ingrid, and I would scoop up the bundles of down from the core, and take them to the South Sea Barn. At the barn we tipped out the messy down onto corrugated-tin drying racks. Each handful brought inside became a mark on the beam next to the date. And, with each nest brought in, the season wound down.

We spent many days walking around the island finding and clearing the emptying nests. Hours and hours out on the skerries and islets. It was often dirty work.

Anna grumbled when she came across a particularly messy nest – the down clogged to the seaweed, sticky with egg goo, littered with fragments of green eggshell. She would pick out the dirty dummy egg with its string and anchor pin, and stuff the messy cloud of down into a plastic bag. In the barn, we would tease the biggest bits of broken eggshell out of the down and toss each fragment in a bucket of rubbish. It was like picking dried pasta out of cotton wool. Sometimes, we'd find whole abandoned eggs. These we buried, to stop predators getting a taste for them.

~

White butterflies shimmered across the purple phlox behind the house, and brown and grey moths rose from the grass as Ingrid passed on her way to the sea barn for the scythe. She cut the grass between the patches of flowers and beamed with delight when I carried on the work later that day, while she and Anna rested. Without any cattle or sheep grazing these island meadows, the grass grew deep and clumpy. Anna told me that, once, some of these islets had been for the sheep, others for young cattle. The milk cow stayed on the hill behind the house and was milked in the Summer Barn. Anna said sometimes the other cattle had swum back across the water to eat the hay meadows around the barns.

We rowed out to South Island one day in mid-June, and Anna found two nests that she hadn't realized were there. She added them to her scrap of paper.

A short-eared owl glided gently over us, its wings a mossy gold in the morning sun. Its mate hopped up from their nest and stared at us from atop a rusty old drum.

~

Day by day, our harvest in the barn grew, and, slowly, the work tipped into a new phase. It was time to begin cleaning the eiderdown whilst we sat at the end of the house in the hot sun.

Ingrid fetched the dirty nests from the South Sea Barn to where Anna and I sat. Anna taught me how to clean the down. She tipped it out of the plastic bags on to the table in front of us, and we pulled any big debris from the bundles, like bits of shell or twig.

The next stage involved a smooth stick – a length of dowel – that they pushed through the down until it looked like a puff of grey candyfloss. Anna and Ingrid danced the bundles on these wands, so that more bits of rubbish fell from the weightless cloud. They were using the nature of the eiderdown to help them. The feathers had tiny hooks that just about held them together, while alien objects that weighed more fell into the cheap plastic buckets between their knees.

As the rubbish fell, it tried to pull the bundle apart, so they used their free hand to pat it back together. Eventually, any remaining fragments were buried deep inside the bundle of fluff. The women felt in with their fingers and picked out each tiny, hard piece of debris.

Next, Anna took a bundle of down to clean using a wooden harp. She set the bundle on the row of cat-gut strings, which were stretched taut across a timber frame the size of a dinner tray. With the harp lying across the gap between her kneecaps and the stool, she used a wooden tool, the thickness of a thumb, to strum a tune across the strings. As she did so, they vibrated, sending waves of kinetic energy through the down and shaking any heavier material to the floor. Little black seaweed fragments gathered by her feet.

After a few strums, she would stop and pick carefully for other bits she had spotted – a tiny twig here, a stronger feather-stub there. The harp made the down look fuzzy and soft, and full of air. It spread across the strings and through the wires with every strum, clinging to itself by its minuscule barbs, caught between falling and holding to the mass. Strum and pick, strum and pick, for maybe twenty minutes. And then Anna took it in her clever, fast hands, and ran it between her fingers, feeling for more grit.

Ingrid and Anna showed me how to use the harp. I was a little awkward to begin with, but soon I was strumming it confidently, the vibrations passing through my knees. I got excited at how perfect the down now looked, and Anna smiled and said this stage was only the crudest of cleans.

The buckets slowly filled with sticks, straw, shards of seaweed and eggshell, and little bits of plastic string that the ducks had woven into their nests. Wisps of down floated in the sunshine around us. The bundles of down warmed in the sun, until they felt alive to the touch.

Days were filled with this work. Once the women had taught me to do it, we sat, busy alongside each other, lost in it. Sometimes we chatted, or swapped notes about what we could see out at sea. Sometimes Anna or Ingrid would just look up from their work and soak in the beauty around us, and then they'd smile at me, catching me looking at them.

Two butterflies danced above the women as they worked, and landed from time to time on or around them. Ingrid said she was always amazed that they crossed the ocean to the islands, when the faintest wind could blow them far out to sea.

After the first cleaning of each bundle of eiderdown, Anna pressed it into a cardboard box. She laid a sheet of magazine paper over it, pressing her hand down on the crosswords and puzzles, or the smiling face of a celebrity. A mark was scribbled in biro on the box lid – IIIII – so they would know what its contents were back on Vega. This was Anna's system, and it was not to be messed with.

~

We talked for hours as we cleaned the down. I asked Anna how many nests she'd managed to get on Måsøy. She said that after fifteen years there had been sixty nests in total. This was an important milestone – sixty nests producing just about enough to make a duvet that could be sold. Almost as an afterthought, she added that she had built up to fifteen nests in duck huts on the main island, along with a scattering of wild nests, too.

I wondered if I had heard her properly. This seemed an absurdly small payoff for so many patient years. But it was, in fact, a huge achievement.

Anna had proven that it was possible to re-establish trust with wild ducks, and to rebuild a duck station – the very thing everyone had said couldn't be done. She had done this against the widespread decline of seabird numbers, in an age when everything was against her. If she had carried on her work on the island, Anna explained, the duck station would have grown – she had done the really hard bit. She had learnt from her efforts, including from many mistakes, and she was a skilled duck woman now, coping with whatever nature threw at her.

It was always tough-going, though. The year she got to sixty nests, an otter went on a killing spree from hut to hut, biting and shaking the ducks until twelve were dead. One of those ducks had been nesting in the same place for four years and was a favourite of Anna's. Building the ducks back up was like that – you thought you were winning, and then it could all unravel. Establishing hundreds of ducks on an island was the work of lifetimes.

Ingrid told me later, when we were alone, that what Anna had done was bigger than restoring her own island – she had helped make something else possible: the revival of other duck stations. It was a small but radical act that had changed the story of the islands to one of hope. When the archipelago became a UNESCO World Heritage Site, there had been a short programme on TV about the duck islands, and it had featured Anna. Afterwards she received a letter addressed to the 'Queen of the Birds', and the man who wrote it said how much he admired her. Anna had been thrilled by the letter until she saw the return address on the envelope was for the local lunatic asylum.

~

Anna was never boastful, but I could tell she was proud to have carried the torch. One afternoon she showed me her traditional dress, and a photo from when she had met the Queen of Norway. There had been an event at the museum to celebrate the World Heritage status. The politicians had dominated the agenda, and had blathered on in their speeches, while the duck women – placed in a line at the back of the room – barely got a mention. Eventually, it was the Queen's turn to speak. She said how happy she was that the work of the eiderdown women was being recognized, at long last. Afterwards, the Queen ignored the agenda and the bigwigs and stopped to talk to Anna and the other women. The old stigma and snobbery against the island people was turned on its head that day. Anna couldn't help but think how proud her grandmother would have been to see it, after all those years of sitting at the back of the church.

~

We now spent much of our time cleaning down and chatting in the sun. The women taught me more Norwegian words, and I watched the sea with my binoculars. A white boat with sport fishermen passed in the distance, a mile or so away, their thin graphite rods standing upright in racks.

Anna and Ingrid moved their chairs round the corner of the house to where the sun shone. One afternoon they had a glass of wine, and sat enjoying the sunshine. I teased them, saying they looked glamorous, like a couple of 1950s movie stars.

The starlings whistled and screeched at us all day long from the ridge of the roof above the veranda. Every few minutes the birds came with their beaks crammed to bursting with earwigs, beetles, and other insects from the undergrowth. The starlings didn't go far, mostly to South Island, where they landed quickly and scurried through the undergrowth, grabbing their food until they could stuff in no more. Several times a day, an earwig or beetle fell from a beak to where the women were sitting. They swept them from their wool or their table. I scribbled down observations in my notebook.

Anna heard a faint chirping sound and wandered off to the gooseberry bushes. She came back and told us the eggs there were hatching. The ducks needed to be left alone so we went inside.

~

That evening the island was peaceful. We were all together in the kitchen doing the simplest of things. Anna was squirting mayonnaise onto tinned mackerel in tomato sauce, on a flatbread, when she looked up and said,

'A whale.'

She said it so simply, before crunching her food, that I wondered if I'd heard her correctly. I peered out. A giant black fin was carving the sea into mouth-sized pieces. I was speechless. I'm not sure what shocked me more, the black back and dorsal fin rising above the water, or Anna's apparent indifference to it. She looked back at me and shrugged, like they came every week. The killer whale appeared uncannily oversized cruising round the little bay – so big it filled the window.

Anna sipped her tea and said plainly, 'And another.'

More members of the pod, some smaller and younger, appeared one by one round the headland in single file. The smaller whales swirled and splashed, like they were playing, their slick backs glistening out of the water. The first whale tipped up like a swimmer doing a handstand at the shallow end of a public pool, and its tail waggled above the water. Ingrid said it was hunting for halibut in the bottom of the channel. Anna said the halibut could be huge.

'Is he the male?' I asked. Anna said she thought so. I wanted to be closer to them, so went out and down the path. The first whale came around the bay, big, black, and long, with booming, masculine breaths like a bull.

Listen to me.

Hear me.

See me.

Einstein worked out that giant objects in space exert giant gravitational pulls, bending the very fabric of space around them, powerful enough to bend time and light. The bull whale was like that. Even the birds had stopped singing. Every creature on the island was spellbound.

My eyes had only been for the first whale, but I saw there was an even bigger whale in the pod – hanging back in the deeper water near the main channel. Anna, now by my shoulder, said the bigger whale was the grandmother. I imagined that she was calling them back, cross that they had gone into the dangerous tidal places. Soon enough, the other whales turned and followed her away to deeper water, occasionally stopping to breach over each other. They disappeared around the headland of Crow Island.

The whales had supercharged the place, electrifying each inlet they passed.

'There must be enough to eat, this is good,' Anna said. She said she had begun to worry they might never come back.

She went in to finish her supper. I climbed the hill and

saw the pod hunt around the inlets and skerries for seals. Soon they were a mile away, in a large bay to the southwest. They hunted for an hour or more in the long, grey twilight, slapping their tails, perhaps to stun herring. Occasionally one leapt out of the water and splashed heavily down.

I had rushed out without a jacket and the cold sea wind began to chill me. I left the whales out there in the evening light. When I passed over the hill and looked down, the bay below the house was still. The water there was slick and flat, like it was spent.

Anna was doing the washing up in the plastic tub in the sink. She told me she had watched a TV programme about orcas once. The females stopped having children in their forties and had a menopause. But after that they often led their pods for decades, sometimes until they were ninety or a hundred years old. With a grandmother watching over them, the pod was safer and lived longer. Someone had to remember where you might get beached or stranded. When a matriarch died, the pods often struggled – the group broke apart or got into trouble, and mortality rates rose. Even the strong, older males saw their life expectancy shortened when their mother and grandmother weren't there. Anna said this pod hunted all along this stretch of coast. That they were perhaps the very same whales she'd seen as a child, or their kin.

6.

An Outing

I had become used to our little island world and its certainties. So I was surprised when Anna announced one morning that she and I would go to the tern colony to the south of Fjærøy. I had forgotten that she'd once roamed further across the waves than she did now. And those places seemed to be calling her, literally: we could hear the birds screeching when the wind was blowing the right way. Anna had decided that, with me as a shipmate, it might be possible to get there and back. Ingrid said she would stay home and cook a hot meal.

As we walked to the jetty, Anna told me that she wanted me to understand that the eider nests were just part of what was once harvested. I had spent the past few weeks doing just one strand of the old island way of life, the eider-duck work, but in the past duck stations were situated among islands with thousands and thousands, sometimes millions, of wild seabirds nesting. A good share of the islander's diet, and their harvest, was taken from these places, and their ethics about what, and how much, could be taken were never stricter than when they were gathering wild eggs. Anna's earliest island memories were of gathering seabird eggs and timber from these wild, rocky places, with the sky full of seabirds all around her and her father. When she heard the screeching of the terns she seemed to decide that she must go again, one last time.

~

She pulled the engine to life, steered us out of the inlet by the sea barn, and navigated the channels to and fro, further and further out into the sea estate. The outboard engine purred and pushed us across the glassy surface of the water. The vast, blue sky above was marked only by an occasional cloud.

The bow wave sent out swells to the foreshore and then ripples shimmered back. Rocky headlands created invisible currents that were made known to us only by seaweed trails, or when our boat was unexpectedly pushed out a few yards into the middle of the channel. After each narrowing there would be a calm little bay or inlet where the water was still and a shade of indigo blue. Anna scanned the foreshore of each island we passed for driftwood. Two or three times she put me ashore. I would clamber up and grab a piece of sawn pine timber – a 10-foot-long bit of 2x4 – as clean and new as if we'd collected it straight from the DIY store. Had they tumbled off a cargo ship? Or washed down a river in a flood from someone's building project? How long had they floated on the waves?

I read the familiar name of an English hardware chain stamped on the timber. Anna said, 'It's your rubbish, right?'

I nodded. The Gulf Stream sweeps north past Britain and up this coastline, and carries with it any rubbish that blows from our shores, flows down our rivers, or falls from our ships.

We soon got to the flat island swathed with green and yellow roseroot where the seabirds nested. Anna pulled the boat up close and dropped the chained anchor in a crack in the rocks. Hundreds of terns and gulls were already above us, a swirling, screaming tornado of seabirds stretching up and up to the heavens. The island was no more than a foot or two above the waves, just far enough to be safe for nests. Anna grabbed my arm and pointed down to where I might otherwise have stood – three eggs were nestled in a scratch in the sand and rocks. Brown and green speckled. Tern eggs. Their nests were everywhere – among stones and broken seashells, between the flat rocks: tiny, crude collections of sticks or a few stones on the bedrock. We trod around them. Terns dive-bombed us and screeched.

Anna walked quietly across the islet. I reached down to touch some eggs, and she stopped me with a wave of her hand. She said it would show the gulls where the nest was, and we must not do that. The ground was littered with smashed and broken seashells, that over time had worn to a gravelly white sand between the rocks. And grey and white feathers lay everywhere. The birds above seemed to make the whole sky revolve, like it might lift us up and away.

'We must go now,' Anna said, 'or the gulls will rob the terns' eggs. We must let the terns protect them.'

And a few seconds later we were pulling away from the nesting place. The afternoon sun was fierce, burning our cheeks. Anna said she had seen enough nests with eggs in them to feel happier about the state of things. There were a lot of eggs.

We were soon far out on the water beneath the bluest of skies. As we sailed away we talked about the sea. I said it was hard to worry about something that looked so perfect, when we could not see below the surface or see the damage we had done. Anna looked at me and was solemn. Nothing was quite the same as it was in the old days, she said. The giant seabird colonies to the north were one by one falling silent, as the birds failed to breed. But, she said quietly, we must not give up.

~

Halfway across to the next island, the engine coughed, spluttered, then stopped. After some cord-pulling and cussing, Anna said we would have to row home. I grabbed the oars, and she sat watching whilst I took us back. She trailed her fingers through the water and peered into its depths. I let the boat glide between strokes. The light flickered and played tricks in the water. Fish flashed and turned from our boat's shadow, twenty feet down. The ocean bed would vanish in shadow and darkness, and then reappear as shallow slabs of rock or banks of white sand. Seaweed ribbons reached up from their anchors on the rocks – a swirling mix of browns, reds, purples, and oranges in every feathered shape. The seabed in 3D, and alive – not the dull black mat laid out on the rocks that it became at low tide. Round the final headland, we passed through a jungle of dark kelp. The oars caught a little at each pull. Then Fjærøy was before us once more. That oasis of human life out on the wild ocean, surrounded by the vast panorama of the coast. The moment was so pure, so simple, and so perfect I wanted it to last forever.

Human life is full of projection, like we are constantly being filmed in the movie of our own lives. We endlessly shape and reshape our own stories to make ourselves feel relevant or seen – desperate to be the major character. But we don't end up feeling seen, we end up drowning in noise, because everyone else is as desperate to be heard as we are. The world has become a mad shouting match, making us distracted and anxious. I'd done all these things as foolishly as anyone else, and it was exhausting. I was just another male duck huffing and puffing on the foreshore.

Anna, by contrast, simply morphed into her surroundings, into the world she had chosen. She wasn't interested in projecting how important she was. She was whatever was around her, whatever she was doing, whatever filled her eyes. I would ask her thoughts about something, and she would shrug and point to whatever the ducks were doing on the foreshore. Her meaning was clear: focus on this world instead, on what is, not on what you think about it.

Anna was not a poet. She rarely explained anything in more than a few words. Her poetry was her life, her work, and the depth of her love for the islands. She didn't give a damn what anyone else thought, or whether they listened to her. Either you tuned in and became part of her world, or you remained an irritant, a jarring note. It wasn't that she had no ego, but that she mostly forgot about it, or shelved it, when she was on the island. And in this radically pared-back life, she had found peace and meaning. She was the waves, the light, and the terns rising and falling on the bay. She was them, and they were her.

She was the guardian of this place. Everything around us, between ocean-bed and sky, was under the protection of this seventy-year-old woman. I looked at her in the boat with me and marvelled at the ridiculousness of it. She was powerless against the scale of the natural forces at work on the islands, and against the issues affecting the oceans, yet fierce in her determination to try.

I could not imagine her leaving this behind. But she smiled at me, her fingers dangling in the water, as if reading my thoughts. I sensed then that this really was a goodbye. She seemed calm, accepting of her fate. The past few days she had confessed to feeling a little tired. She looked at me, rowing gently, and said that getting old was not a thing you could beat. She said you could be braver than a rough night in a storm, but ageing was relentless, like the waves wearing away at the rocks. She was not sad to be going back.

The island was not her whole life, just the place where she spent each spring. She would tidy her neglected garden at Steinbakken. After her divorce, she explained, she had moved into the white house her father had built. The house that she had resisted moving into as a child was now, I realized, her home.

~

I had been deeply affected by Anna's love of her family's island. For decades, it had been the sun around which her life had revolved, and the work she had done there was her greatest triumph. Every time I'd asked her what had happened to the family island – asked why she was no longer there – it was clear she didn't want to tell me. I wondered if something had happened with her brother; maybe life on Vega was just easier if you buried old feuds. But now, she told me the barest of facts.

After her father died, Anna and her siblings had agreed that she would continue running the duck station on their family island. Her brother Tore would come back to live on Vega, and look after the island the rest of the year.

For a few years, it worked out – until, one day, it didn't. Tore had gone back south to his wife and children, and couldn't be on Vega as much as he'd planned. It was then he announced that he would come each spring and take over making the nests. And so, after fifteen years of work, bringing the duck station back to life, Anna never went to Måsøy again.

She fell silent. Perhaps she saw the look on my face. I couldn't believe it. I felt heartbroken for her, and then, as I thought about it, angry. She had devoted her life to that island, and then it seemed to have been taken away. I wrestled with what Anna told me, trying to understand it, but she was not for explaining, and Tore was not here to ask. We docked back at Fjærøy and returned to the house.

~

That night I lay awake in bed reading *The Odyssey*. I hadn't slept well for days. The blanket I'd hung as a curtain against my bedroom window could not keep out the Arctic light.

Strange fears rose inside me. Minutes took hours to pass. My brain seemed unable to stop racing, so much so that I became scared of it. It was like a printer gone mad, churning out reams and reams of gibberish. I was sweating. Years of stress coming out of me like poison.

I dressed and went down to the living room. In the mirror, I was shocked at how much older I looked than earlier in the day. The man looking back at me was grey. My eye sockets had become shadows.

I went out into the light.

At the top of the hill, the scene before me was like a

Turner painting. The giant orange sun blazed low on the horizon as if someone had opened a furnace door. It filled the tidal place with colour, turning the sea to fire. The back of the white house was bathed in warm orange light. The herringbone sky painted red and yellow. I sat on a rock surrounded by the sea and thought about my life, all that had passed, all the people I had loved who had now gone. I missed my father, my grandparents, and a whole tribe of people I had known and understood. I felt as though I had only existed as a reflection in their eyes. I had been keeping everything going, loyal to their world, and their values. But what did that mean when they were gone? My grandfather would scarcely have believed that the most common of birds in his fields would vanish, that the commonest of sounds, like the curlew, would not be heard. The silence filled me with shame. I had friends that would pretend nothing had changed: the fields were still green, the soil still brown, the river still ran to the sea. They acted like everything could go on as it always had. But that made no sense to me. I felt confused, lonely, and out of time.

When my mum had told me I had inherited my dad's shotgun, I'd had to gently decline because I was scared of what I might do with it.

I had buried my grief for my father, buried my feelings, buried myself under work and striving for years, and now an earthquake was rising in me, raw and uncontrollable. I had come here seeking solitude, when all I had done my whole life was isolate myself. I thought being here would teach me how to tough it out on my own, how to be an island. But there was no escaping other people, no escaping pain. I sat and cried. Seabirds on the skerries to the north mewed and screeched, the tidal channels flowed out fast, and the two old women in the house lay sleeping.

~

In the morning the light was bright and clean. Anna noticed I was quiet and asked what was wrong. I said I was feeling a touch homesick. She said I should be homesick – my life was a good one, I was married to a good woman and had four lovely children. She was pleased to hear I missed them. She told me I should be with my family, and would be again soon. But not just yet, because she needed me here, and she wasn't about to call Henrik for an evacuation.

I had assumed that Anna had always loved being alone on the outermost islands. But she told me, 'It is not so great being alone, when you want to be with your people.' She knew island life better than anyone else, and understood that escaping to an island to get away from other people was just a fantasy – and a lonely fantasy at that.

She said that during her first season on Fjærøy she had been really homesick. She'd brought rugs and carpets and new curtains with her to make it feel more like home. But it wasn't her island, and she'd felt isolated like never before.

To this day, she'd often go up to the top of the hill behind the house and look through her binoculars to see her home on Vega. She couldn't see it through the forest that had grown up around it since her childhood, but she pretended she could. From that hill, she could see an island mountain of Søla, on the back of Vega, and she knew that behind that was Måsøy.

She told me her brother had carried on making nests there. As she said this, I was surprised by the lack of bitterness in her voice.

~

The days of checking every nest every day for new birds and eggs were over. There were not so many new ducks coming now, and we sensed that certain huts and nests were unlikely to be used, so the rounds grew shorter. There might be another week or so before we headed back to Vega, Anna told me.

One morning, we discovered that the duck that nested in the ravine close to Crow Island had left without hatching her eggs, simply leaving them to go cold. She was the first of several birds to do so in those final few days. Perhaps they were unsettled without their mates, or by another duck leaving. Or perhaps they were unsure about being mothers. Perhaps they were just too hungry to stay any longer.

Sea-mayweed rose, daisy-white and yellow, from the cracks on the rocks, and wild pansies trembled in the breeze. Rock pipits flitted down to the seaweed, piping for their chicks. A mother goose climbed the rocks on Crow Island and was followed by three half-grown goslings. The mother raised her head to look for danger.

~

Anna walked down one of the paths and spotted a duck hesitating to leave the shelter of a bush with her six ducklings. Anna walked a dozen or so strides past the bush and then turned to look back and watch. The mother duck was following her down the path, calling her ducklings to heel. She took a few more steps, and then stopped, and the mother duck followed, then stopped, as if she and her brood were playing grandmother's footsteps. The duck knew the dangers of taking six ducklings across a headland to the sea with so many gulls, crows, and eagles around, so she was following Anna.

Anna saw what was happening and changed her course – turning off the path and straight to the shore. At the high-tide mark the mother duck took her leave and her ducklings vanished into the seaweed and rocks, safe for now.

With every passing day more ducks got their ducklings away. As they went, the responsibility Anna felt to them passed into memory.

~

Just as the ducks brought the magic to the island, they took it away with them when they left for the sea. The males were long gone, and now there were barely any females in sight. The island felt like a cinema five minutes after everyone else has left: strangely empty, with a kind of after-buzz in the air. There was the sense of an ending, but this show wasn't quite over. When we left, the work wouldn't be completely done. There would be a final trip in late summer to tidy up and deal with the last nests. And the eiderdown would need to be hand-processed at home in the barn, again and again, to be perfectly clean for selling. Some of the duck women worked on it until Christmas or after.

~

As we passed into the final island days, the half-idle atmosphere of mid-June was replaced by hustle and bustle. There was a sense that time was now finite again, and the work left substantial. The living room was often empty now – the women were outside finishing this and mending that, cleaning and packing and storing. Piles of wood were thrown out of the barns, and taken to other places to be cut for firewood, or saved for nest-building the following spring. We almost trod on the land rats on the paths; they were getting fatter and we were getting quicker. They scurried away just far enough to believe themselves hidden, but often left half their bodies in sight on the edge of the path, their coats dark and sleek and damp from the grass. The cow byre next to the house was cleaned out, the finished and unused nests cleared away from the alley and swept up, and the worn wooden floorboards appeared again. The cod that Stig had split to their tails and hung on the fish rack at the end of the barn were now curling round their stripy skins, their tails flapping to the sky.

The house smelt of cleaning fluid, the mop, and dust and dirt being shifted. Ingrid spent an afternoon on her knees cleaning the kitchen floor until it glistened. Anna laughed when she saw her. 'Don't get so close to the floor. You will only see the shit.'

Many of the pictures, books, and household items didn't belong to Anna, so she would leave them. Old pieces of furniture that Anna had never liked were brought back in from the barns and put in the bedrooms; Terje's house returned to the way he liked it.

The rugs were lifted and beaten against the barn until clouds of grey dust coughed out of them. Anna unscrewed the old CB radio from the wall with the cordless drill. As each screw fell out it hung a little more crooked. No one used two-way radios any more. Sometimes she talked of 'next year', like she had forgotten that this was supposed to be her last year, and I'd catch Ingrid looking at her.

After our evening meal, we sat in the living room. The

sky lifted and lightened behind the women as they knitted on the sofa. Elvis was crooning out 'How Great
Thou Art' with a gospel choir. In the back garden the
purple phlox swayed gently in the wind.

~

Anna and I combed through the gooseberry bushes and
taller island vegetation for nests we might have missed.
A duck rose in front of us and flapped away. 'Ah,' said
Anna, and she sent me for tissues. The duck had shit on
the eggs in her panic, and we were to clean them up. I
bumped into Ingrid, carrying an unused nest box. The
roof was rotten, she said, the duck who came to it every
year had spurned it this time round. It must have a new
one fitted, she said.

She handed it to me and I knocked in the old roof,
peeling off each fragment of rotten plywood. Then, with
the claw hammer, I pulled out all the nails. I laid on some
old, white-painted rails, nailed them in place, and sawed
the excess off.

When I showed the women the nest box, Ingrid was
not happy with my crude work. She and Anna had a
confab about its shortcomings, and Anna went into the
barn for a better, waterproof roof. After some clanging,
she came out with a length of shiny corrugated tin,
already cut to length, and laid it on the top. Ingrid hammered in the tin nails and bent in the corners and the
sharp edges. Then she took it back over the hill to its

ledge, replacing it exactly where it had always been. 'She will have a better home next year, and I think she will like it,' Ingrid said to Anna.

~

Ingrid would not talk about the time after Anna, but I sensed that she wanted to be the next duck woman now, more than anything. When she was young, she told me, she hadn't known this work was an option, or she might well have chosen it and lived a different life.

Anna seemed half relieved that Ingrid wanted to care for the ducks – she knew that her friend could do that now – and half anxious that the future would include Ingrid's husband. She didn't like the idea of a man on the island. I sensed in the final week or two that Ingrid had edged away a little from Anna. She looked less to her for approval, and spoke to her more like an equal. She seemed to have one eye on a future without Anna in charge. I think they both knew things could not be the same, the dynamic would change, and it might not be comfortable for either of them. Perhaps islands are like farms, almost impossible to pass down the generations without someone getting hurt. We cannot be what we are and what we aspire to be at the same time, something in us has to die for something else to be born.

~

The geese idled in the sunshine, grazing the summer turf. They waddled with their yellowy-downed goslings up out of the water and through the rocks and seaweed. As nests were cleared and huts dismantled, whole head-lands and outlying islands could be forgotten about. I'd see the raven or the eagles sitting in those places again now.

We would not go to Ship Island again. The work there was done, the nests that were occupied had hatched and been cleared. Our fears of otters and mink receded. We saw another Arctic skua fly over the area, but ignored it. The ducklings would already be out on the sea. We could do nothing for them now.

~

Anna sat at the table with her hair loose, wearing a cream and grey patterned woollen jumper, red pyjamas, and knitted purple socks. She wrote her final entry in the nesting diary. Of the 121 used nests, ninety-eight had been harvested for their down. Thirty-six of those had been crudely cleaned. She thought there were twenty-one birds still sitting. Several ducks had abandoned their nests, leaving cold eggs behind. Anna said the birds were acting differently to how they used to, when she first came.

On one phone call, she'd heard that the same thing had happened on Flatholm. Anna wondered if the ducks weren't as fat as they needed to be. The scientists had been weighing them and realized they needed to come ashore in good condition, nice and fat, to endure the privations and stress of laying, sitting, and hatching their chicks. If they came in from the sea lean, then they could not endure the hardship of sitting so long on nests, which often cost them 30 per cent of their body weight. When the ducks abandoned their nests, as sometimes happened, they were perhaps simply worn out and hungry. The worsening feeding conditions for the ducks out at sea in winter were playing out on the down islands in the spring.

Once she had finished with the diary, Anna said we must empty the little red house today, and blushed. They never called the compost toilet by its real name. We went out and lifted the old rotting planks and sheets of damp plyboard where they had buried the latrine the previous year. The 'night soil' beneath was almost black now – finger-thick worms wriggled inside. There were still some bits of sawdust in the soil, and green eggshells. We dug a fresh hole among this deep soil, around two feet deep and three or four feet long, like a tiny grave, stopping when we hit the bedrock. Anna decided it was too windy to continue, so we left it for an hour or two. Later the women went back and finished the work without me, out of modesty. They buried the waste beneath a layer of soil and I helped cover it up with the boards and timbers.

'I do not need a water closet,' Anna told me. 'I think this is better than chemicals and soapy water.'

She checked the ropes that tied the toilet down through the winter storms. She always tried to leave the island in better condition than she found it. 'Terje's family might come to spend their summer holidays here in July,' she said. It would become their place again. It struck me then that neither Ingrid nor Anna would be the ones to decide who came next year – the future of this duck station was in Terje's gift.

~

Henrik would come tomorrow, Anna said. There was one last job she had been saving for as late as possible – a final trip to South Island and South Rock to gather the down.

I rowed us across. We made the huts and the stone houses there ready for winter, storing the wooden fronts from all the nests inside the huts, away from storms. Anna used a rope to tie down the corrugated-tin roof of a hut, anchoring it around some boulders. Then we loaded the boat and I rowed gently round the whole headland and to the wharf for the last time. The blue sky opened out above us. The little white house shone on the now glowing-green island. Close to us there was a splash, like someone had thrown a pebble into the sea, and then out of the splash rose an Arctic tern, shaking itself up into the sky.

When we got back to the wharf, Anna climbed up and took the last bag of down with her. Henrik could tow this little boat home now. 'Though we must tell him to go on half-throttle, or all the timber will end up in the sea,' she said.

We walked past the house and across the island to mark the final nest score on the wooden beam with a black marker pen. The roar of the distant ocean waves could be heard at the edge of the sea estate. Half a dozen gulls were held on the wind, frozen in time above the island, as if caught in a photograph.

~

Ingrid made our last supper. Fishcakes, caramelized fried onions, potato wedges, and a mountain of pancakes. We stuffed ourselves with the pancakes, heaped with blackberry jam and brown sugar that crunched between our teeth. Anna said that in his prime Henning could eat twelve pancakes, then laughed. Afterwards, I washed the dishes and tossed the soapy water from the decking onto a patch of nettles. The women sat on the sofa, knitting and talking. Anna kept glancing out to the sea.

An hour or two later we ate a platter of cheese with salty Ritz biscuits, and grazed on peanuts, and slowly emptied the red-wine box on the sideboard into small, transparent beakers. The wine made us giddy and at bedtime we ate the last of the cold pancakes. The phone rang, and Anna talked to her daughters. Yes, we were coming home tomorrow. Yes, she was OK. Yes, she would bring his rifle back. Ingrid said she must get some sleep, and the floorboards were soon creaking above us. Anna followed her upstairs.

I should have gone to bed, but felt that I might never return to this place, I walked outside. The island was a deep, dark green now, the meadows rank with cocksfoot, reed grass, and billowing clouds of meadowsweet that turned silver as the wind passed across it. The island was waiting for us to leave, to become wild again. And, now, I was ready to go home. Like Anna, I had a place to care for, and it was time to go back and do that.

~

I slept like the dead and woke to the sound of the waves and the wind, and the seabirds to the north. I gathered my things and stuffed them into my holdall. When I went downstairs, all the pots and pans had been washed and stacked away. The bedding was bagged up by the door. The cushions on the sofa were plumped.

The women scurried here and there in a wordless rush, quite convinced they didn't need me, except to carry the heavier things. It was like they had remembered I was a man, and it went without saying that a man would make a mess of packing.

Anna stuffed her boots and coats into black plastic bin bags. Then filled another bag on the table with her kitchen things. Floorboards creaked. The door-catch clinked and clanked as they came and went. Questions flew from one room to another. Where was this? And where was that? A growing mound of bags occupied the hall: Anna's canvas suitcase, a plump red rucksack, and the big, square repeat-use shopping bags packed up with the dry goods from the pantry. Cheese, milk, and eggs were packed into cool boxes for the journey home.

Ingrid put back the scythe and I gathered up plastic buckets and containers and stacked them in the barns. After an hour or two she said we must pause, or we would all be worn out. She made us a drink and we sipped from small, white coffee cups. Three ducks paddled out into the bay, trailing a V behind them.

Ingrid shuffled the yellow generator back into the porch and I lifted it into its cardboard box. The gas canisters and fuel were stored in the barn. Anna wrote her name on them with a marker pen, in case Lars fancied using them. I was tasked with moving grey roofing sheets to the edge of the wharf, pinning them beneath rough timber and rocks. Anna tied the plastic waste beneath a green canvas sheet for the conservation officers to collect with their boat. The pile was now the size of a family car, and we had only collected a small share of what lay around the shore. I pushed the loaded wheelbarrow down the path and over the wooden walkways, through the banks of water avens with their hanging pink and purple heads. My grandmother, I remembered, called these flowers soldier's buttons.

To and fro we went, to the wharf loaded with black plastic bags, tubs full of food, the down harp, the rifle, the eggs, and the eiderdown. The living-room floor was brushed and mopped until the linoleum shone and the house echoed.

~

We stand in the kitchen, like three strangers waiting on a platform for the train. We are ready too soon, and hang about aimlessly, listening out for the sound of Henrik's engine. Not really living, but caught between lives.

It is no longer our job to heed every screech and whistle of the seabirds. The empty headlands are no longer our business. The purple phlox behind the house looks past its best. And the flowers on the headland have closed their buds like they are not for us any more.

The spell is breaking. Our island family is coming to an end. For a moment, a feeling of alienation, of being a stranger to these people, returns to me. I feel daunted by going home, by trying to make a better life, one that won't weigh quite so heavy on my shoulders.

Anna's thoughts seem to be on her garden at home, the barn renovations she has planned, and seeing her family. Ingrid, too, looks to be thinking of her home life with Stig, and perhaps a future in which she comes back here with him next year. And I become lost in thoughts of seeing my wife and my children, and writing the next chapter of our lives together.

I go to the back door. Low, grey clouds crawl in over the ocean. I stare across it for a glimpse of Henrik's boat. Anna goes out the front, and a moment later we hear her say, 'Quick, come outside.'

On top of the red barn are eight or nine redshanks, the whole brood now fledged. The two women stand and look at them, smiling.

Anna says, 'They have come to say goodbye,' and the island echoes with their calls.

~

The island and the wild things are never fully known. There is no end to learning. Anna knows that, and, now, so do I. When we were young, the old folk seemed to know everything. I had imagined that there was a moment when you felt wise, that you had learnt it all. She looks over at me, smiling, as though she can hear the thought. We are all just children. We never know enough, not even the half of it.

7.

Home

As we sailed back into the harbour, Vega glowed a luminous green. The snow had long gone from the mountains, and the trees, now in full leaf, reached up the rocky screes. The blue sky was broken only by the contrail of a jet. Everything was bathed in the most brilliant sunshine.

Henrik and Anna chatted all the way home. The tensions between them on the way out, seventy days earlier, had melted away. At the harbour, he offered to help Anna haul her stuff inside the sea barn, but she ushered him back into his boat. Ingrid had to get home because she was going to a party later that afternoon. Stig was waiting for her behind the boathouse in his pick-up truck. He waved at me, and I smiled back. We loaded Ingrid's things in the back of the truck. Then, at the last moment, Ingrid grabbed Anna and hugged her tight. Anna looked like she might cry, but, instead, she squeezed her, and said 'Thank you.' Then they were gone, and Anna and I were alone.

Anna locked the door of the sea barn and we walked up the gravel track to the houses. She said we would come back later with her car for the rest of her stuff.

The harbour now felt crowded with homes, boats, and sea barns. Red, white, and yellow houses arced around the headlands. Farmsteads were scattered further inland, among the greenery. I marvelled at all these people living on top of each other. And with every step up the hill the world felt lusher. Clumps of birch, poplar, rowan, goat willow, and hazel rose on the roadsides and from the rocky headlands. The air was heavy with sap.

We walked up to the crossroads at the heart of the village, past the garage that Anna's sister and brother-in-law once ran as a café and shop. Her brother-in-law was a good man, Anna said. In the early days he had brought groceries out to the island if she'd been short of anything. His shop had been a trove of stuff. Hardware and work clothes and black clogs, overalls and life jackets; fishing stuff like hooks, rods, different strengths of nylon line, and shiny lures that flashed in the water like sand eels. And he sold woollen yarn, knitting needles, and cotton thread. An enormous dried cod hung from the ceiling. He'd insisted it was a hundred years old and could tell the weather by the way it pointed.

It had been in the shop, Anna said, that she had heard that they were looking for another duck woman on Fjærøyvær.

~

Anna thought she was finished with the ducks when she left Måsøy. Her first season back on Vega, she had lain so low that many of her friends assumed she was away as usual.

Life wasn't over, she said. It was just different.

It was the following year that she bumped into another duck woman in the shop. Maren was minding Fjærøyvær, because the long-standing duck woman there, Emma, had retired a year or two before. But she was also getting too old for it all. When she saw Anna was back on Vega, she sensed she might be persuaded. She told Anna the ducks on Fjærøyvær produced about two kilograms of down per year, enough for two quilts. Not as impressive as in its heyday, but still a serious eiderdown island, a respected place that Anna's family had spoken of in the past. Maren knew that Anna could get more ducks to nest on the islands. She asked if she could recommend her to the owner.

Anna didn't commit either way, but was grateful to be considered. The voice in her head said it was a stupid idea. Working on someone else's duck station wasn't the same as following her father and grand-mother. It would be lousy money, and she'd have another man to answer to. They probably did things in different ways to what she was used to. And it would be fleeting. The list of reasons not to go was long. But that night she couldn't stop thinking about it. She would still have to juggle it around her work, but they could manage for a few weeks. She'd gone before, and the world hadn't ended. It was only a boat ride away if she needed to come back. Her girls were now grown up and working in Oslo. They loved her being a duck woman. They could help her when they came home for their holidays. There were masses of ducks on Fjærøyvær, way more than she had worked with previously. Anna argued with herself for days, trying to kill the idea.

Until, finally, she had walked down her lane, turned right, and up the hill to Terje's house. She knocked and was hollered in. He was pleased she had come. And when she came out of his house an hour later, she was the next duck woman of Fjærøyvær.

~

There was something like elation in me as we walked home that day, and I believe there was in Anna, too. We floated happily up the road.

We were now free of cares, our work and duties over – students walking home from school for the summer holidays. The island work was done. The ducks had been helped. They had gone back to the sea with their young. The eiderdown was collected and stored in the sea barn behind us, ready for cleaning. The egg rent was packed, ready for sharing between the old man and the last duck woman. The season, which had lurched so close to failure, had been successfully navigated. Anna's blood pressure had lowered, and she said she felt younger than she had in years. She had accomplished the thing she set out to do.

~

The gardens in the village were full of flowers. I almost sneezed as the pollen hit my nose. Anna nodded to villagers standing on their doorsteps. They looked like they were waiting for something. A woman told her the wedding party was coming. Ah, Anna said, yes, she had forgotten. And then we heard the drums and the chanting coming down a road winding between the hills. The young men at the front were singing an old folk song, and striding out in their best blue, brown, and grey suits. Their polished leather shoes were rimmed with dust. Three or four drummers beat out a crude marching tune. The bride hitched her ivory dress up off the road. Her shoulders were draped in a turquoise embroidered cardigan. She had flowers in her blonde hair that matched those in the verges. Soon she had her arms round her new husband and one of his friends, and they swung her off her feet every few steps. Behind the couple and his best man were fifty or sixty of the bride and groom's kinfolk and friends. The bridesmaids and the bride's friends were all in pretty pink and cream dresses, with more wildflowers tucked in their ponytails or woven into their plaits. The young men at the front shouted, adding hurrahs into each song, or bawled out the choruses in response to the lead balladeer.

They had come the mile or so from the bride's childhood home and were heading to the restaurant on the headland where the evening meal and dancing was to take place. The bride lived and worked far away from the island now, and her husband was from somewhere else too. But she was still loved here, in this island community that had raised her. She was Rita's daughter, Rita from the museum, Anna told me. The groom put his hand up to demand they change song, and shouted its title. They all laughed and protested at his poor taste, and then joined in and sang it anyway. A dog on the other side of a picket fence yapped and raced alongside the procession, until it reached the end of its garden and could only bounce and whine in the corner.

Anna watched the young people pass with a smile. Some of them waved when they saw her, and she waved back. She told me she knew these young women from when they were girls. Then she saw Mari, halfway down the procession. Her blonde hair flowed down her back, and she was clutching tight to her red-haired boyfriend, Erik. Mari waved to Anna with a big smile that said, 'I love you.' One song ended, and the music stuttered a little until the drummers found their beat. Mari shouted, 'Don't wait up for us coming home, Mother.' Anna shrugged at me, and chuckled. 'That's going to be messy,' she said. 'They'll get drunk.' And then Mari was swept round the corner with the crowd. Some of the older folk at the back were in full traditional costume. They stumbled along, chatting loudly, like they had been drinking already. And then the last of them was gone, and the dust began to settle.

Anna and I looked at one another. I think we'd both felt the magnetic urge to follow the party. All that love and fun was intoxicating. But when the last echo of the crowd was lost behind the wooded headland, the moment passed. The wedding party left behind a wake of elderly smiles and chattering on doorsteps, and a few wilted flowers lay in the dust, where they had fallen.

~

I was thinking about my own life as we walked, and the choices I had made. I asked Anna if she had any regrets. She thought for a moment, then said that if she could go back and do it again, she would live every single day of her life exactly the same the second time round. The staying on Vega when the others left for work in Oslo or the mainland. The men she'd loved and lost. The baby sick, the dirty nappies. The scrubbing of pots, and the cooking. The job in the old people's home. And the slog and the joy of the duck islands. She said she'd do it all again in a heartbeat with no regrets at all.

I asked if she'd miss the island work. She tilted her head and smiled as if to say yes, and no. She had lived it all, the sweat and dirt, the nest-making and clearing, the killing mink and otters, the dead ducks, the storms and blizzards, the boat journeys across the waves, the bad years when it felt futile and the good ones when it felt like a dream. Anna didn't do regrets. The story was not of her leaving, because someday everyone must leave, but that she had gotten out to the island at all.

~

On our final evening on the island I'd seen Anna staring out the back window. The setting sun had given the island a golden halo. She said she had once seen a giant woman gazing out from the hillside there. Anna had gasped and clutched her hands to her chest. She re-enacted that for me, looking like a medieval peasant who had seen a saint. I asked if she was scared and she said no – she had felt calm. She described the *huldra* as having beautiful hair, lots of it, high eyebrows, huge eyes, a fine nose that turned up a little at the end, and strong lips and a long neck. She was like a carving of a woman on a ship's bow. And then she had gone. Anna had never seen her again. But a few months later, when she was cleaning the house up, she'd found the sketch of a woman beneath one of the beds, the drawing I had seen on the living room wall. She knew it was the same woman she had seen. Anna asked Terje who did the drawing, and learned that a son of the family who'd been on the island almost a century ago had done it. It was said he had been lured into the earth by the *huldra*, seduced, but came to at the last moment and yanked free. Anna looked to me earnestly and said,

'I do not think she is bad . . . I think she is good. She cares for this place. I think the *huldra* lived on the earth before us, and then we took over, the bad people.'

It seemed to help Anna, knowing that she had left the island, and Ingrid, in the care of the *huldra*. A person's life is not so long. Humans come and go. But the *huldra* live in almost geological time, much longer lives.

~

We followed the road, heading further inland, past a lawn mower abandoned mid-job on a stripy lawn. Anna said her garden would be a tangle of weeds. We passed open fields, and she swung her arms, carefree and happy, her rucksack hanging from her shoulder. The road turned through wooded hillocks. In the verges, cow parsley filled the air with the smell of aniseed. The headlands around us were jewelled with birdsfoot trefoil, daisies, pink campion, and buttercups. A curlew stood on a telegraph pole silhouetted against the sky. Three more fed on a field with their long, curved beaks.

The radio mast on the mountain beyond the village caught the sunshine. Plantations of spruce below formed a dark-green backdrop to the farmsteads. And beyond the trees was the rocky, wild end of the island, where Anna told me she would soon go gathering cloudberries with her daughters. Last year she'd wandered up one of the ravines on her own and had found so many berries she'd been picking for hours. Her daughters had been frantic when they found her, thinking she had got lost or fallen. She'd been wearing a green coat, which had made her vanish into the background. But she was just fine, and teased them for worrying.

~

My notepad was stuffed away in my bag, my scribbling done, but I could sense that Anna wanted to tell me more. Memories tumbled out of her. She told me that, in the long summers of her childhood, she and her brother had run wild across this end of Vega. One night they took the family rowing boat out to go fishing, she and her brother. Her mother wailed after them not to fall out of the boat, but they ignored her and raced down the dusty lane. They fished until long after midnight in the Arctic twilight, her brother rowing them round the headlands. In a greasy, flat patch of ocean, they caught lots of pollock. They yanked them into the boat, and carried them home through the fields by their gills. When they got into the kitchen their father was in his pyjamas and vest, smiling with pride. He pointed a finger upwards, and then to his lips to make them be quiet. Then he fried the fish in butter for them all, whilst their mother slept upstairs.

~

We walked past a red barn on the corner and got a whiff of slurry from the pigs. Anna met a neighbour on the road. They chatted as they walked, about nothing in particular. Then the neighbour was gone. Soon Anna could see her home. The mown verges were now yellow with dandelions, like quick daubs on a van Gogh painting. And a small flock of kittiwakes passed over, riding the gentle sea breeze across the island.

'There's my brother's house,' she said. His rubbish bins had been put out. Her own empty bin had blown onto the track. We set it back up. The white clapboard of her house was bright against the spruce plantation behind it. Anna's ginger cat appeared at her knee and meowed at her, and she meowed back. We were now on her property, with its rickety wire fences. The posts and rails caught the sunshine and shone silver. The elder-flower bushes on the bank by the lane were laced with creamy white flowers. When I'd first come here in late April, I had not known Anna's brother lived so close. Nor had I noticed how beautiful Anna's home on Vega was. Her face lit up with a smile as we approached.

A speckle-faced sheep and two lambs skit away, then stopped, looking at her guiltily. They rattled through the rusty wire and ran into the grassy yard. Anna found the key in the secret place where she'd left it. She dumped her rucksack at the back door and went into the quiet-ness of the house. In the kitchen, she lit a cigarette and stood at the window.

~

Anna watched the lambs playing, racing round their mothers and skipping and kicking their legs in the air.

On the dining table, her potted plants were coming into flower. Outside, the lawn needed mowing. The rhubarb was waist-high and ready to be harvested with a knife.

This was a moment of time unfilled – a vacuum. The responsibilities of the island were now miles away. The responsibilities of home had not yet crowded into her head. It would be a few hours before all of her neighbours and family realized that she was back; no doubt they'd come to see her tomorrow. She sat and drank her coffee and breathed it in. The clock ticked away in the otherwise silent living room. The cat climbed over her knee and pushed up into her as she stroked his arched back. I went out to mow the lawn, and she watered the plants on the windowsills and dining-room table.

~

Anna washed her work clothes, pulling them from her bag onto the floor, and then running them through the washer in batches. She said she would put mine through too, so I put a pile by the machine. They smelt damp, of duck shit and the black earth of the island. Anna turned the dial, poured in the powder, and set off a wash. She told me to make myself at home in the room I had used before, and, whereas I'd felt a stranger the last time I'd stayed here, I felt like family now. On the stairs I passed framed photos of her sons and daughters, brother and sister, and her parents. Halfway up, I saw twenty-year-old Anna on the stairs – a picture of her from 1969. She was blonde, with piercing blue eyes, in a floral V-neck dress, her hair set and sprayed firm in the style of the day. The young woman in the picture looked defiant. Anna had hinted that men had always wanted her. Perhaps they'd sensed they couldn't have all of her. She wasn't anyone's pushover. She looked tough, like she had her own ideas. Young men like that, until they get married.

~

Everyone leaves their island in the end, Anna said. Some leave in a box, but most leave when they can no longer do the rough work and cope with the rigours of island life. Anna's grandmother and father had both left when they were old. She had satisfied her island longing, done her duty, and now the past had to be let go. I sensed, then, that in the early days of this season she had been wrestling with this ending, and had eventually found some kind of peace in it. It was almost like she had done a deal with the gods – 'Let me be well enough to do this season, and I will leave with grace.' The gods had let her recover and enjoy those weeks, and now she would keep her end of the bargain.

Her father had not been so lucky. He had worsened in the nursing home. He often came to the kitchen when Anna was working. He stood behind the big can-opener that was fixed to the worktop and used it as a ship's wheel. She'd be chopping vegetables, or washing up, or cooking, and then notice her father was navigating between two skerries out at sea. Sometimes he'd wander off from the nursing home. But it was a small town and he'd be recognized going down the road. He told whoever stopped him that he was going to the boats, and he'd be gently brought back.

Sometimes he'd go with her when she went to tend the family graves. One day, she'd been on her knees, scratching away the leaves, and he'd looked at her and the gravestones, and said, sounding like himself again, 'There is not much point to this work.' And Anna and he had laughed together, because it was true.

~

Anna and I both woke early the next morning, at 5 a.m. She had, she said, slept deeply, beneath her own eiderdown duvet. She made scrambled eggs and brown toast and black coffee. She sat in her chair by the window and watched the light on the trees.

Sometime later, Mari and Erik stumbled in the door, whispering to each other before they realized we were awake. They were doe-eyed with tiredness and drink. Anna made them breakfast. They told her this and that from the wedding, and she told them little things from the island. They were staying home for a couple of weeks for their holidays. Mari sat on Erik on an armchair and teased him for being so 'tired'. And then they went to bed, and Anna washed up.

We got in her little twenty-year-old red car and drove down to the harbour to collect Anna's things, retracing the route we'd walked the day before. It took three journeys to get it all home. On the final journey, she placed the box with the eider eggs packed for Terje on the front seat. She would take them and pay her respects later, if he was well enough for a visitor. Someone had said he was in the hospital, but she was not sure this was right.

She asked me if I wanted to go with her to Henning's farm to take his rifle back. We took the winding road across the island. Past the woods and fields. Through the tiny town of Gladstad. Past the supermarket. Past the giant, white wooden church where her family were buried. I asked her about Henning, about what their relationship was like. It was fine, she said. I joked that driving to her ex-husband's house with a rifle might not end well, and she laughed it off.

'It was a long time ago.'

We drove on, through the wild, scrubby places and woodland, to the flatter part of the island where she had once lived. She said Henning worried about her having his gun. It wouldn't look good if she was caught with his firearm. He fretted, so she always took it back as soon as she could. I'd assumed they had very little to do with each other, but she told me they sometimes went to Oslo together to see the girls.

We pulled up the drive to his house, past sheep nibbling away at the bare turf.

As we walked up to his house, Anna told me she gave him her only eiderdown duvet when they parted.

'You let him keep your only eiderdown duvet?'

'Yes,' she said. He had helped her a lot on the island, and continued doing so, in his way, even after their divorce. Besides, it didn't matter too much, she said, as she knew then she would soon have a new one from her nests.

Henning still came for Christmas dinner. Anna was like another grandmother to his younger daughter. She was a good kid. Anna lifted the gun out of the car. 'Come on,' she said.

Henning took us in and we talked. Anna went to put the gun away. I was surprised by how warmly I felt towards him. He was a quiet and thoughtful man, and just a few days earlier I had cast him in my head as a jerk. Anna's stories had affected me; I felt angry at anyone that had ever hurt her. But now it was old news. Anna was at peace with all that had been, and that was enough for me. I told him about the seabirds I had seen, and he said there used to be way more. He had made a wooden nest box for the black guillemots, because Amalie loved to see them on the wharf on Fjærøy. He said his girls could take it and fix it up there. The more we talked, the more I saw how kind and good a father he had been. A story is rarely as simple as it seems. We are all a bundle of virtues and vices, strengths and flaws, hopes and fears.

Anna told Henning to come round later, as 'everyone' was coming for a bite to eat. She told him to bring his youngest daughter. He mumbled thanks, and said he would come. We headed home.

On the way back we stopped at the Spar in town, and stocked up on supplies. I noticed some women were watching us from down an aisle. I asked Anna what they were gossiping about, and she said, 'Oh, word has gotten around that I had a younger man on the island. They probably think we are having an affair.' When I asked if that was a problem, she smiled wickedly and walked a little closer to me until we got to the checkout.

~

Back in the car, I remembered a story Anna had told me about her first husband, Bernt. One spring, after he and Anna had separated, and he was living up on Svalbard, he had found some abandoned eggs under one of the diesel generators near his room. The mother had left them, but the warmth of the engine meant they had hatched. Bernt took them in and cared for them. When they got bigger, they'd paddled round on the pond whilst he worked. Then, one day, they'd gone to sea, and he'd felt proud to help them, but life had felt emptier. He told Anna and their sons all about it when he came back to Vega. He showed them cinefilm he'd taken: polar bears and Arctic foxes, and then his ducklings.

It struck me that Anna's life was full of people, mostly men, who had loved her deeply, but who had let her down or hurt her. As she'd told me their stories, I had assumed she'd cut them out of her life, been as savage as I was to the people that hurt me. But I was wrong. She had forgiven them all, both for being what they were and for what they'd done. She had woven her family and her tribe back together. She had a lasting impact on people, even on those who had gone their own way. Bernt had cared for those ducklings, and had come back to tell her.

I had been drawn to Anna because she seemed heroically tough – and she was tough, but her real superpower was forgiveness. She knew that a life full of other people meant accepting their weaknesses and still being there for them. I had mistaken Anna for a loner. I thought she had gone to the island for the same reason I had: to get away from others. And perhaps she had, but the truth was that she lived surrounded by people who loved and admired her. With hindsight I could see that the island had been a revolving door of other people drawn to her, just as I was. The lesson she taught me was not about toughing it out. Or being as harsh and judgemental as an Old Testament prophet. She was showing me that a good life was about forgiveness – accepting others' flaws as we hope they might in turn forgive ours. Anna showed me how much we all need each other, and how empty it is to be alone.

I had been driven to the island by anger, I realized. I had been most angry at those closest to me – bitter that no one seemed to recognize the trouble I was in, that no one was helping me in quite the way I needed. But Anna had worked out that letting go of anger was not just an act of kindness to the other person, it was kindness to yourself. Holding on to hurt eventually burns a hole in you. Forgiveness gives everyone a chance to do better next time.

~

It was late morning when Ingrid's car came down the lane. She parked on the grass by the red barn. She had woken up missing her friend, she said, and squeezed Anna's arm. Anna poured her coffee. We sat around making small talk. Ingrid said Stig had decided not to sell his beautiful boat for another year or two. He loved it too much to give it up just yet. I wondered if this was code for Ingrid having gone to see Terje, and being named the next duck woman on Fjærøyvær. But by now I knew both women well enough to understand they would never speak openly about it. What would be would be, and I would learn about it when the time was right.

Ingrid said the women at the party last night had flocked round her to ask about the islands. Everyone had said how well she looked. Ingrid glowed with happiness and health when she came back each July, and it fascinated them. They compared their suntans to hers and peppered her with questions. The other women had rarely been to the outermost islands. She told them it wasn't really that far. You could see her house from the island with binoculars. She told them there was a house, a stove, a fridge (when the generator was on), and comfortable beds. She told them that we'd sat and eaten good food and sometimes enjoyed a glass of wine. That we did the washing up, just like at home. But she could see in their eyes they thought it was a kind of fairy tale.

~

There was an hour or so until Anna's friends and family were due to come, and the two women decided to make the barn ready for cleaning the down. We tidied the middle loft and swept the wooden floorboards. The eiderdown was laid out on racks. It would all be cleaned again and again until it was perfect. Anna told me that, in the old days, the buyers would pay less if, when they bounced the down above a mirror, any dust fell to the glass. Ingrid said that they worked on it every spare minute they had. Somewhere down the line there would be a quilt. Anna thought there were fewer than twenty quilts a year now made and sold this way. She wanted both of her daughters to have one. Ingrid hoped she would be able to do the same for her daughter someday.

~

One of the most surprising things about Anna was just how many other people she had inspired. Surprising, because she had little interest in recognition or praise. But as the years passed by, more and more people had noticed and come to respect what she was doing. Norway had become one of the richest countries on earth. Many of its citizens wanted to know about their past and about life on the islands. They were amazed that some of their ancient traditions were still alive. What had once been mocked as backwards was now admired and respected.

Schoolchildren were being taught about island culture

in their classes, and sometimes the museum would ask Anna to help with a workshop, making nests – although there were too many cats and dogs on Vega for those nests ever to be used. Occasionally, other women would come and see Anna working on the island. There were all sorts of practical reasons for going to see her: she, of course, knew a lot about the ducks and the nests and eiderdown. But when I spoke to some of those women, later, it seemed like they'd gone to see Anna because they were searching for something. They needed to see a woman who had done it. She gave people courage to be more than they had yet dared to be, just by being herself. If she could live out there and make it work, then so could they. She had kept alive what their grandmothers had been, carried the torch long enough for others to take it from her. She had also been one of a small group of determined people, mostly women, who had made UNESCO recognize this seascape as a World Heritage Site. It would be strange to describe Anna as a spokesperson for the duck women, because she preferred to say very little – but the other women knew that if they needed to convince anyone about the duck tradition and why it mattered, you took them to Anna's islands to see her ducks. It always worked. She'd even cropped up in meetings as far as away as Trondheim, when they needed her magic to win over politicians or civil servants. The government's top bird scientist met her in one such meeting and was in awe of her. He had studied on the islands as a young researcher, and had learnt a lot from Anna's father.

It could be traced all the way back to a moment of rebellion in a small care-home kitchen. That squabble about time off work had been like a tiny pebble thrown in to the stillest of lakes, it set off ripples that spread and spread.

~

Anna and Ingrid walked down the ramp of the barn, and across the yard to the house. Anna turned to me and said, 'Come on, we have done enough work.' It was time to go and set up the food; everyone would be arriving soon.

I stood for a moment and looked to the rooms where she had lived as a child. I thought about how she had come full circle, back to the place where she had been born. I had followed her far out to the edge and back, this island woman twinkling with magic. For the past thirty years, she had been casting a spell on one person after another, causing them to care about the ducks. When they built a beautiful new museum on Vega to celebrate the eider-down tradition, a photograph of a duck woman's gnarly hands adorned with her rings, cupping an eider duckling, became the iconic image of this whole archipelago.

~

Anna carves some salmon on a little cutting board. Mari comes into the kitchen. Ingrid gives her a hug. The younger woman squeezes her arm. We hear Anna's son, Erik, rumble down the lane on his Harley Davidson. He walks through the door, looking like he could fist-fight the local police in a parking lot, but his eyes smile kindly when he asks his mother how she is. He gives her a cuddle. He quizzes me on what I have learnt from his mother, and tells me proudly his memories of her as a boy. He asks her if the plants he watered are OK. And tells her the cat has gone wild and thinks it owns the place. He says the damn thing meowed at him every time he stopped by, like it thought it was a tiger.

Anna's brother-in-law appears below the kitchen window – he chops a few of the logs, and then is in the kitchen and apologizing for not getting the pile chopped before Anna got back. You split them when you get time, and I'll stack them in the shed, Anna says. And then he is gone. Half an hour later Henning arrives with his youngest daughter. He sits quietly in the chair in the corner. Mari gets them both a drink and a slice of cake. The young girl comes to Anna and whispers something. Anna cuddles her and goes to get some sweets. Then, after a while, they too went home. A few minutes later, Amalie rings from Oslo, and Anna speaks to her in the hall. After a while I hear her say, 'You must speak to your new brother from England,' and she passes me the phone.

~

The door opens and Tore, Anna's brother, walks in. I am surprised to see him, though perhaps I shouldn't be. He takes a seat. I sense that he has been worried about

Anna, but he avoids the subject of the duck-station work, and doesn't really know what to talk to Anna about after a couple of sentences. I tell him we saw whales, and he responds with a tale of a time he saw them, too.

It was a Sunday, and he had taken his little boat out from Måsøy. It was high summer. Blue skies. He felt tired, and had done his work for the day, so he flicked off the engine. The sea was still as glass. He scrunched up his coat and made a makeshift pillow and lay on his back among the ropes and nets. Sometime later, he awoke with the strange feeling that he was a baby again, his parents peering into his cot. But a strange clicking noise was pulsing through his body. He slowly focused his waking eyes on a dark movement alongside the boat and met a shining, big, black eye. A whale's nose bobbed, black and white, and wet, alongside the little boat. It was staring in at him. He wondered if he was dreaming. Then something moved behind him, on the other side of the boat. When he turned there was another whale, bobbing and peering in. He thought later the whales were perhaps talking to each other, deciding whether he was food, but they were gentle and he wasn't afraid. He rose to his elbow and became a man. The whales dropped into the depths. He sat up and saw that he had drifted perhaps half a mile from where he had been when he lay down. He looked at his watch and found he had been asleep for two hours. His cheek was burnt from the sun.

He heard the water swirling round the boat, and saw he was close to a seaweed-covered reef that barely cleared the gently rising tide. On the last few inches of rock was a seal. It looked at him like a sad dog. Then two whales rose next to it and a little bow-wave swept across the rocks. The seal shuffled submissively to the edge and plopped into the sea, where three or four giant shadows were waiting. Then the shadows became fins, and the bodies of whales, that churned the surface of the sea white with their swirling tails. They grabbed and ripped the seal to pieces. Tore sat frozen still in the rocking boat as the sea around him turned red with blood. And then he was alone again, except for the screaming of a hungry herring gull or two.

~

As Tore is telling this story I begin to think about our power over nature, and its power over us – about the forces that swirl around us. I think about the whales Anna and I had seen, about the matriarch and the bull. And the seal in Tore's story plopping into the water to be killed. I think about why I had come to this place so far from home. I had been searching for an escape, a place outside the broken world. I had been searching for a hero, and I found what I'd thought was the most defiant person alive. But, instead of a superhero, I had become friends with an ordinary woman who had lived an extraordinary life.

Along the way, as I had heard her story, I had been angry at this brother of hers. In the kitchen, chatting to him, I realize I am still cross, but at myself, for making old mistakes again, and still not truly understanding. Other people's disagreements are not mine; I will never know what happened. I will never know who said this, or did that, or what flaws this person, or that person, had. Anna has been trying to tell me this for weeks, encouraging me not to judge others so harshly. She said to me one day on the island that the details of what had gone on between them were just 'tittle-tattle'.

~

I hadn't known it at the time, but a certain version of me died on that island – a person who had been quite effective and ruthless, a machine-like me that got things done in a machine age. I was returning different, like I had been reassembled, or born again, to use that strange Christian phrase. I was looking at the world differently and thinking about myself differently. I stopped feeling like I had to tough everything out, to prove myself to the world. I still wanted to honour my father, but I stopped feeling bound by his memory to act in a certain way. I did not want to be the same person I'd been. It was time to lay down a lot of baggage I'd carried for many years. It was time to stop striving and being so single-minded. And it was time to forgive myself for having been all of that, for I had not meant to hurt people. Now, I just wanted to get to work with my family; to make our farm the most beautiful and abundant place it could be. And then, when my time was up, I would know I had done my best. I would have lived like Anna.

Anna's example was simple: if we are to save the world, we have to start somewhere. We just have to do one damn thing after another. Hers was a small kind of heroism, but it was the most powerful kind. The kind that saves us. We all have to go to work in our own communities, in our own landscapes. We have to show up day in, day out, for years and years, doing the work. There will be no brass band, no parade. And we have to accept and keep the faith in each other, and somehow work together. It is the only way we can make our own tiny deeds add up to become the change we all need.

~

When Anna's family had all gone home, she washed up, and I carried the last cups and plates to her. She nodded out of the window to a roe deer and its fawn in the grassy hollow before the spruce plantation. The fawn was so young it barely knew what its stick-thin legs were for. Its roan coat shone bright in a patch of sunlight. Anna put away the drinking glasses in the side cupboard. When she came back to the sink, she looked out again, and the deer had led her fawn back into the shadows.

A Word on the Text

One of the strangest things about the eiderdown tradition is that there are no widely agreed upon names for
what to call things in Norwegian, yet alone English
translations. On the islands where it happened, it was
simply part of people's lives. Outside those places few
people knew about it or talked about it. So no one
today is quite sure what to call the people who care for
the eider ducks. Various terms get used: 'duck ten-
ders', 'duck wardens', 'down wives', or 'egg and down
maids'. None of these seemed to translate very well
into English, so I took the liberty of using a simpler
term for Anna – a 'duck woman'. The same applies to
the places where the work took place, sometimes
referred to as 'egg and down islets' or 'egg and down
rookeries'. I have called them 'eiderdown stations' or
'duck stations'.

~

Readers should also be aware that this book isn't history
or biography, with all the sources and footnotes such a
thing would require. It is simply a story about one spring
on a duck island, told from the memory of a stranger.
Names and descriptions have been changed to protect

people's privacy. This book isn't the full or final account of anyone in it: they should tell their own stories, and I hope they can in the future. The judgements of character within it, or any mistakes of understanding, are fleeting ones from that specific moment in time, based on what the stranger – me – saw, heard, and believed to be true. I have sought to tell it all as I understood it at the time.

Since the events in this book took place, I have been welcomed to a number of other duck stations, and seen the amazing work being done in those places by dozens of fine women and men. I hope some readers might support their ongoing work, and the little duck station in this book, by considering a donation to help fund restoration work and training future duck people – https://verdensarvvega.no/donations.

~

On one of the many days on the island, when it was raining heavily and we had no choice but to retreat to the fire and drink coffee, Anna asked me if I would write a book about her and what kind of book it would be. I answered that I wasn't sure, but that if I did, I would write about her work, her island, her family's story, and her own life. I told her I could never know the whole of her, another human entirely, a woman, and someone from another culture to my own – such a thing was probably impossible, but if I did write an account,

I would try to make it as true as I could. I explained that I was trying to see the world through her eyes. I would probably try to make of her life a kind of fable. I asked if that would be OK, and she said yes.

I am only the storyteller. She is the story.

Acknowledgements

A massive THANK YOU to:

Anna, for being yourself, sharing your life story despite being very modest, and for being kind to me. If this tale has any merit, it is because I captured some of your spirit. We laughed all the time on that island, and I'll always be grateful for it. If the details are wonky, blame the strange Englishman for misunderstanding. Ingrid, for your friendship and taking me fishing.

Thank you to everyone on Vega – the warmest and most decent people I have ever had the pleasure to get to know, each and every one of you. Profound thanks to my closest Norwegian friends for helping me try to understand their world.

Peter Debrine for sending me to Norway the first time.

Rita Johansen for making it all logistically possible. Martin Skjefstad for putting up with a lodger.

Bente Sundsvold for her PhD and film about the tradition, which were valuable sources, and for her insights, when we briefly met in Bodø.

Jim Gill, my long-suffering agent, for selling this book while I was in Oslo airport. And thanks to the rest of the team at United Agents.

Chloe Currens for buying the book while I was in

Oslo airport. But, more, for being the best editor in the business, and one of my dearest friends.

Anna Fletcher for inspired help when we needed fresh eyes. Stefan McGrath for backing me behind the scenes. And Ingrid Matts, Rosie Brown, Alba Ziegler-Bailey, and Pen Vogler, and all the other Penguins for all your work.

Thank you to Jane Clarke for being the most wonderful reader and friend. And thank you Vanessa Kissule for your careful reading.

Molly, Bea, Isaac, and Tom, for managing without your dad for a few weeks, and filling in for me on the farm. And for all the days when your mum and dad are up in the office trying to turn thoughts into scribbles into stories.

And Helen Rebanks for trusting me when I started spending our savings on random flights to Norway for a strange project that might have gone nowhere, and being there every step of the way since. But mostly for loving me.